Physical Education in Primary Schools

Access for All

Elizabeth Knight and Sue Chedzoy

David Fulton Publishers
London

David Fulton Publishers Ltd
The Chiswick Centre, 414 Chiswick High Road, London W4 5TF
www.fultonpublishers.co.uk

First published in Great Britain in 1997 by David Fulton Publishers

Note: The rights of Elizabeth Knight and Sue Chedzoy to be identified as the
authors of this work have been asserted by them in accordance with the
Copyright, Designs and Patents Act 1988.

David Fulton Publishers is a division of Granada Learning Limited, part of
Granada plc.

British Library Cataloguing in Publication Data
A catalogue record for this book is available from the British Library.

ISBN 1-85346-491-0

Typeset by Sheila Knight, London

Contents

Acknowledgements

We would like to thank St Sidwell's Combined School, Exeter and Vranch House, Exeter for enabling us to take photographs of children in action. We are indebted to Anita Davidson for her constant support in preparation of the manuscript.

Introduction

Aims and purpose of the book

For many primary teachers who do not have a Physical Education specialism the Physical Education (PE) lesson can be a daunting experience. For some, their lack of subject knowledge and uncertainty of how the children will respond in the more open situations beyond the classroom mean that many may feel very insecure, deskilled or inadequate. Sometimes a naughty child within the class lesson can be the eagerly awaited opportunity for the teacher to cancel the scheduled hall or outside games lesson.

This book aims to consider some of the possible reasons why the Physical Education lesson, although adequately planned, can go disastrously wrong, leaving the teacher feeling that he or she has lost control. The focus will be on children who do not do as they are told or what is being asked of them within lessons. The possible causes are investigated.

In most cases it can be seen that the demands of the lesson are often inappropriate for some children and, because of the nature of their difficulties, can cause a negative ripple through the class. How children behave/respond will be a key focus. The links with coordination difficulties and associated problems thus preventing these children from meeting the demands made of them will be expanded.

This book is about helping teachers to:

- identify strategies for including children with coordination and associated difficulties within Physical Education lessons

- identify different types of Special Educational Needs (SEN) and how these affect children's ability to respond in Physical Education lessons

- provide activities and individual educational programmes for pupils with specified needs.

The book aims to guide the inexperienced, unconfident teacher when taking class Physical Education lessons and provide useful information in order that the pitfalls are avoided. It provides examples of how teachers within Physical Education lessons can be more successful in providing for children with special needs.. Much of the material is presented in a form which is transferable to overhead transparencies in order to facilitate Inset for teachers, advisers, lecturers in Initial Teaching Training and parent support groups.

Chapter 1 provides an opportunity to reflect on the environment in which PE is being offered and invites readers to consider where they are in this process. Three strands are discussed:

- School policy on Physical Education
- Teacher as manager
- Children's individual needs.

Instances of ineffective lessons which all teachers, however experienced, will recognise are also included in Chapter 1 with some identified reasons for their occurrence offered. The need to recognise Special Educational Needs in relation to PE is highlighted.

Chapter 2 considers current legislation and offers guidelines for including children with more obvious identifiable special needs. Reference is made to safe 'inclusion' (*Safe Practice in Physical Education*, BAALPE 1995). However many needs which are physical in nature are not always recognised. In order to do this teachers need to:

- observe children working
- analyse tasks and situations.

Chapter 3 therefore provides detailed analysis to enable teachers to gain skills in recognising some of the difficulties children might have. The different aspects of analysing movement and relating these to the Programmes of Study for Games, Gymnastic Activities and Dance are considered.

Chapter 4 provides stepping stones or progressional markers to enable those children whose difficulties stem from movement limitations to have access to the Physical Education curriculum. Special consideration is given to children with behavioural difficulties. The role of support in relation to the Code of Practice is also considered. A summary of the skills needed by teachers catering for individual needs is included.

Chapter 5 looks at accessing the curriculum for children with SEN within lessons.

Chapter 6 looks at individual educational programmes for children with identified specific needs and suggests remedial programmes which may be incorporated within whole-class situations. Individual programmes which can be used as a back-up are provided to enhance specified areas of weakness. Activities for addressing some problem areas conclude the chapter.

Chapter 1

The Effective School Environment

> The successful Physical Education lesson where all individual children's needs are met cannot be seen in isolation but must be considered within the context of the whole school environment.

The diagram on p. 2 looks at the vital components in facilitating this.

Each facet needs to be considered and each of the following sections of this chapter could be used as a checklist for teachers to identify where they are, or their school is, within the whole process. The points made for each section are perceived from the standpoint of Physical Education.

Points **highlighted** (i.e. in bold type) are deemed to be of greater significance for children with special educational needs.

Reasons why lessons are not always as one would wish are related to some school-based research findings. Some possible causes are offered.

Good practice in Physical Education

The school
Broad, balanced curriculum
Relevant documentation
Procedures for reporting
and recording

**The effective school
environment**

The teacher
Effective manager
Sensitive communicator
Good analytical skills
Sound subject knowledge

The children
Experiencing and
enjoying the programme
Improving skills
Feeling valued

Accountability
National Curriculum
requirement
OFSTED
League tables

Support and development
Governors
Community
Other agencies
Health Service

The school

> A good school is where all people feel able to communicate, share information and act upon it appropriately.

A good school will have:

- Managers who are flexible and adaptable and recognise strengths and problems.

- An ongoing development plan.

- Clear written policies for all areas of school life.

- **A coordinator for Physical Education and a coordinator for Special Educational Needs who communicate with each other.**

- **Studied the Code of Practice (DfE 1994) and be aware of the implications for children who experience difficulties in Physical Education.**

- **A support mechanism for children requiring extra provision.**

- **A governor with responsibility for Special Educational Needs.**

- An appropriate provision and sharing of Physical Education facilities and equipment.

- Accepted rules and established routines.

- An ethos which encourages caring and sharing, responsibility and respect amongst everyone.

- **Good home–school relations.**

- **Communication with outside agencies.**

Which of these features are in place in your school?

The teacher as manager

A good teacher–manager maintains order and provides a safe environment where children can be purposefully active.

This will involve :

- Organising children to and from the working area.

- Establishing a shared and recognised routine with all staff and children within the school.

- Knowledge of subject matter.

- Organising a safe working area with appropriate boundaries.

- Planning lessons and units of work relating to the whole school scheme and National Curriculum requirements.

- Checking that the equipment and apparatus is accessible and ready for use.

- **Being sensitive to children's varying needs.**

The manager will need to:

- Provide opportunities for keeping the children physically active through a range and variety of appropriate tasks.

- Create opportunities for children to plan and evaluate their own and others' performance.

- Encourage children to stay on task and work independently.

Which of these aspects have you addressed?

Which are the areas that need further development?

The children

A good lesson is one in which the children respond according to expectations and where there is an interaction between them and the teacher.

To achieve this:

- **Match the task to children's needs. This involves knowing the children's potential strengths and weaknesses.**

Children will need to:

- **Experience success.**

- **Acquire a foundation of basic skills and have their previous experience of physical activity recognised.**

- **Have attainable goals.**

- **Know and understand what is expected of them.**

- **Be taught how to work within a group and with others and have opportunities to be sensitive to the range of movement activities of other children (e.g. through partner work, cooperation).**

- Have opportunities to plan and evaluate their own work and the work of others; this involves allowing time and opportunities for questioning.

Are these in place for your children? How do you know?

Most teachers recognise these as components for success but the reality may be hard to achieve.

The diagram on p. 6 summarises some of the underlying causes why children's individual needs may not be met, resulting in a mismatch between teachers' expectations and children's performance.

Why can't they?

School policy?
Curriculum – no guidelines
No support
Inconsistency in sanctions, standards
and procedures
Resources – inappropriate or insufficient
Facilities – cramped indoor space, no hall
Limited outdoor space, no field

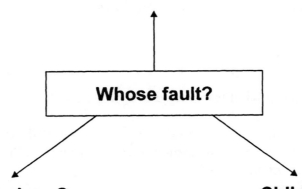

Whose fault?

Teachers?
Lack of confidence
Limited subject knowledge and
progressional markers
Difficulty with planning and
management skills (see
'The teacher as manager')
Inappropriate teaching styles

Children?
Lack of skills and success
Difficulties in learning
Unmotivated, badly behaved

Instances of ineffective Physical Education lessons

The observations contained in the following pages were made by students during their first ten-week school-based experience. These research findings were a result of a questionnaire issued to non-specialist primary students after the ten weeks. In their initial training, at this stage of their professional development, they had experienced a short course (40 hours) in Physical Education addressing Athletics Activities, Games, Dance and Gymnastic Activities.

In other areas of the curriculum children who are unable to fulfil prescribed tasks are easier to recognise with the help of assessment tools. Teachers are more able to identify children's strengths and weaknesses with more concrete evidence on which to base their findings. Since physical activity is so transitory, assessing underlying causes of difficulties can be problematic. There is little or no time to reflect; the pace of the lesson and everyone moving at the same time in a potentially dangerous situation presents problems for teachers. As a result, many children, often have needs which are unrecognised.

Some of the following situations are the result of lack of recognition of some children's individual special needs, which have to be considered in relation to current legislation.

Do you recognise any of these statements?

'Did you observe any poor Physical Education lessons?'

Student observations	Possible causes
'No safety considerations/no specific instructions (children unable to work because too much scope was given, e.g. 'make up a bat and ball game').'	Lack of planning and management skills.
'Larger children made to feel inadequate, e.g. unreasonable tasks, especially in competitive activities.'	Inappropriate tasks. Greater awareness of children's individual needs. Consideration of differentiated tasks. Greater awareness of the range of teaching styles.
'Outside PE lessons were chaotic and therefore not productive.'	Inconsistency in procedures for outdoor activities. Use of boundaries essential.
'The children were left to get out a lot of equipment which they didn't do very safely.'	Lack of organisation and planning. Safety policy lacking.

'The teachers in the school never followed a clear progression of lessons. They would often jump from different activities and not really work at a particular skill.'	Insufficient school curriculum policy. Lack of teacher subject knowledge. Insufficient written guidance and no effective PE coordinator.
'Asking children to choose their own teams and some are always left to last.'	Inappropriate teaching styles, lack of sensitivity to individual needs
'Lack of enthusiasm on the teacher's part.' 'Little or no warm up routines.' 'Poor management of materials.'	Lack of teacher confidence. Lack of teacher subject knowledge. Lack of teacher planning.
'Having to stop the lesson to sort out the materials.'	Lack of organisation.
'Only one tennis ball used with a class of 34 children.'	Insufficient equipment.
'The very able participated in games/ activity: the ones not very good – umpiring, refereeing, goalkeeper.'	Lack of differentiation within tasks.
'I always got the group of weaker children whereas the school team members were all carted off for individual team training.'	Lack of teacher awareness of children's individual needs.

'*Did you notice any individual children who did not do what you or the teacher wanted or expected?*'

Student observations	**Possible causes**
'A child reluctant to get changed for the lesson.' 'Children very reluctant to participate.'	Lack of awareness on the teacher's part of children's individual needs, which could relate to skills level, lack of understanding, fear, level of confidence or competence, self esteem.
'Gave clear instructions "make sure the bat hits the ball with no power" (i.e. object was to make contact with the ball). One or two children hit the ball as far as they could despite me stressing not to, many times. This then resulted in time wasting.'	Children's lack of skill and ability to adapt. Lack of teacher communication skill in explaining reason for a task which the children perceive as inappropriate.

'Misuse of equipment, unequal sharing of equipment.'	Lack of clear guidelines on standards and procedures – links with safe practice.
'Showing off if the child failed to get their own way, either in relation to the activity or group make-up.'	Avoidance tactics, fear of failure in front of peers.
'Children who were disruptive in class were even harder to control in an open space.'	Lack of children's physical skill. No defined boundaries. Lack of awareness of progression. Failure by teacher to recognise children's needs in terms of responsibility and expectations.
'Children who thought they knew the rules and disappeared after disputes.'	Children's inability to work with others. Lack of consideration of progressional markers (see p. 28).
'There were some children who were not keen on PE. They would either forget their kit or suddenly feel ill just as the lesson was to begin.'	Avoidance tactics by children. Lack of skill. Mismatch of tasks to learners' needs.
'Some children who were not very good at PE did not match up to the other children and what I expected them to do at that age.'	Lack of subject knowledge and progressional markers.
'The Special Needs children in the class tried very hard in lessons but they could not do the tasks.'	Teacher expectations inappropriate to children's needs.
'One child was very athletic looking in build yet hated PE because she was so much bigger than the other children. Physically she could have achieved much greater goals but she didn't like to because she stood out.'	Peer pressure. Child's unrealistic self concept.

'One boy hated team sports, he was never particularly social in other classes and at play times. He found team PE lessons very disorientating. He was brilliant at running and could run all day, but try to channel that into, say, football and he kept out of the game as much as possible. He often tried to hide in the toilet during the games lessons. I have no idea how this could be improved, it was very difficult to deal with.'

A mismatch between task and personal needs.
Perceptual difficulties of child not recognised.
Resulting behaviour due to frustration.

'Some children didn't listen to me, but I think it was because they didn't enjoy the lesson.'

Children unmotivated usually because of lack of success in tasks.

'Ben punched Graham in the face.'

Frustration.

'Sports day, some children did not want to take part so the teacher threatened them to make them run. They started crying to me, I don't think children are going to enjoy PE if they are bullied and threatened.'

Inappropriate tasks.
Inappropriate use of competition.

'Were there any overt negative signs to indicate how children feel in Physical Education lessons?'

Student observations

Possible causes

'We had one boy in a wheelchair and children were enthusiastic about having to partner him as it meant they didn't have to take part in the PE lesson.'

Lack of appropriate programme for child with Special Education Needs.
Identifying SEN as needing something different.

'Children not involved in class – very negative attitude, no good at PE, picked daisies.'

Children's self concept and peer pressure.
Lack of children experiencing success.

'Children took a long time to get changed if they didn't enjoy PE, or they simply forgot kit.'

Children using avoidance tactics because they are not experiencing success through appropriate activities.

'Reluctant children always stood at the back of the group and did not *try* to answer any questions'.

Lack of children's self concept.
Possibly inappropriate management and teaching of skill.

'Lack of motivation, reluctance to demonstrate ideas or participate in team work.'

Children's lack of opportunity to develop a repertoire of movement to enable them to take part in team games. Lack of subject knowledge and progressional markers.

'Didn't like being in competition.'

Mismatch of tasks to learner's needs (see section on partner work, p. 56).

'Ben was obviously not very interested.'

Unmotivated child might have SEN – difficulty in concentration. Inappropriate task, unstimulating curriculum material. Failure situation.

'Some children saw it as an activity for the fit. One got a headache at the thought of doing PE.'

Teacher not sharing learning objectives with children. Fear felt by children not used to physical activity (see section on active/fit children, p. 51).

Most of the children had clear ideas of what PE was, so when I varied the games to make it easier for some of the younger children, they were disgusted! This isn't as you are supposed to do it.'

Management skills – sharing objectives with the children and explaining why we do activities.

Chapters 4, 5 and 6 provide suggestions/tasks for rectifying some of these scenarios.

Chapter 2

Who are the Children with Special Educational Needs in Physical Education?

The National Curriculum states that all children regardless of ability are entitled to a broad, balanced programme of Physical Education.

> The revised National Curriculum for Physical Education (DfE 1995) provides teachers with much greater flexibility to respond to the needs of pupils with identified special educational needs. The statement on access in the section on Common Requirements increases the scope for teachers to provide such pupils with appropriately challenging work at each key stage. This should help to reduce the instances where the requirements of the National Curriculum need to be modified or disapplied for a pupil, either temporarily by the head teacher's direction or through a statement of special educational needs.
>
> (Sugden and Talbot 1996, p. 5)

The National Curriculum for Physical Education (DfE 1995) requires that all children receive a broad, balanced and relevant curriculum which is appropriate to their individual needs. The Common Requirements for the Programmes of Study state:

> The programme of study for each key stage should be taught to the great majority of pupils in the key stage, in ways appropriate to their abilities.
>
> **For the small number of pupils who may need the provision, material may be selected from earlier or later key stages where it is necessary to enable individual pupils to progress and demonstrate achievement. Such material should be presented in contexts suitable to the pupil's age.**
>
> **... Appropriate provision should be made for those pupils who need activities to be adapted in order to participate in physical education.**
>
> (DfE 1995, p. 1)

More detailed information about who the children are with SEN in relation to Physical Education was given in the Secretary of State's Proposals for Physical Education (DES 1991).

Children with Special Educational Needs in Physical Education

The highlighted sections in the following statements from the National Curriculum (1991) will provide the main focus of the materials considered in this book. Thus, the needs of children described in paragraph 5 will be considered in greater detail than those described in paragraph 6. However, by considering how to deal with children with coordination problems and associated difficulties specifically, the needs of those with more identifiable SEN as in paragraph 6 will also be catered for.

4 **Since the subject essentially concerns movement, any child who has a movement difficulty can be regarded as having a special need. Such children will include those who have difficulty with hearing instructions, seeing a movement demonstrated, or understanding what is required of them.**

5 There will be some children who have special educational needs in other academic subjects, including some of those who have **formal statements** under the 1981 Education Act, who may not have special needs in physical education. By the same token, **far more children, who do <u>not</u> have formal statements under the Act, <u>will</u> have special needs in physical education. This includes all those children with mild motor disabilities who are sometimes labelled 'clumsy' children, some of whom have recently been shown to have difficulty with coordinated movements. <u>Such problems may also be associated with a range of educational, social and emotional problems including intense personal feelings caused by their perceived failure to move as easily as their peers.</u>**

6 There are, of course, many groups of children who are easily recognised as having special needs in physical education. They include children with sensory impairments, both visual and auditory, those with locomotor and other movement problems, those with severe or moderate learning difficulties, those with medical conditions such as diabetes, epilepsy or asthma, those with emotional and behavioural disorders, and those with profound and multiple learning difficulties.

(DES 1991, p. 55)

Special Educational Needs may be temporary or permanent, mild or severe. We no longer talk about categories of disabilities, rather a continuum of need. However, it is still helpful to think in terms of groupings. The National Curriculum Council's *Physical Education Non-Statutory Guidance* (1992) states in Section E1:

1.3. For pupils with special needs in physical education these may be as a result of:

- sensory difficulties;
- physical difficulties;
- cognitive limitations;
- emotional and behavioural disorders.

A closer look at children with Special Educational Needs

Within each of the NCC's broad groupings there will be variation and a range of individual needs which need to be considered in relation to the task/environment requirement.

Children with sensory difficulties

Degrees of visual, auditory and sensory loss may vary from minimal to total impairment which may be of a permanent, temporary or intermittent nature.

Children with physical difficulties

Difficulties may range from those with specific movement difficulties, which may or may not involve the use of artificial aids such as wheelchairs or callipers, to those with little or no identifiable neurological disorder but presenting awkward movement patterns. The latter group are often described as children with clumsy symptoms or as having dyspraxia. The most recent and formal description of such children uses the terminology Development Coordination Disorder (DCD).

Children with learning difficulties

These children usually have their cognitive needs recognised in academic subjects but such children may experience difficulties within the Physical Education context. Difficulties may be of a mild or severe nature.

Children with emotional and behavioural difficulties

Emotional and behavioural difficulties may be identified needs such as hyperactivity, attention deficit or anti-social behaviour, or may be outcomes from other difficulties such as lack of skill, poor body image, lack of self worth and rejection by others. More often than not these needs are not perceived as requiring special recognition and remediation and thus such children fail to get a Physical Education curriculum relevant to their individual needs.

Guidelines for adapting teaching situations for differing groups of children with Special Educational Needs

For teachers who are aware of those children with Special Educational Needs the guidelines below provide a summary of key points to consider when including these pupils within lessons.

Visually impaired

- Be aware of potentially dangerous objects.
- Enlarge target objects.
- Use brightly coloured equipment and materials.
- Check lighting.
- Modify activities when children change direction – give verbal cues prior to change, e.g. 'Turn to your right in two seconds or when you hear the bell'.
- Make sure the area of work is uncluttered and safe.
- Be consistent.
- Provide structure and routine.

Hearing impaired

- Place pupil where the teacher's or helper's face is visible.
- Establish eye contact.
- Use agreed hand/implement signals (flags, lights) along with verbal commands.
- Use visual demonstrations.
- Encourage pupil to follow other pupils – the 'buddy system' is useful.
- Safety rules should be written and visible to deaf pupils.
- Avoid shouting.
- Remember deaf pupils may have motor difficulties, especially with balance.

Learning difficulties

- Allow more time for learning to take place.
- Reduce the number of activities in which the pupil is involved in the lesson (implications regarding expectations compared with the rest of the class).
- Identify terminology and keep it to a minimum.
- Give one instruction at a time and repeat often.
- Use short sentences whenever possible.
- Break down skills and teach one part at a time.
- Give plenty of praise.
- Use visual and manual demonstrations.
- Always stress safety rules (e.g. 'go' and 'stop' and ways of entering and leaving the work area).

Physical impairment

- Check medical records to make sure which activities a pupil is able to participate in (especially important after illness/surgery).
- Plan for active participation in all lessons.
- Provide frequent periods of rest for those with limited endurance.
- Check area of work is uncluttered.
- Be aware of the correct ways of lifting.
- Teach pupils how to lower body weight safely.
- Teach pupils how to transfer from upright position to sitting/lying position.
- Teach pupils how to transfer from wheelchair to chair or floor.
- Substitute sitting, kneeling or lying positions (balance) for standing positions when necessary.
- Use lighter weight, larger, slower-moving equipment (balloon).
- Teach basic wheelchair skills before pupil participates with equipment in a game.

Safety

Safety is a key focus when considering including children with Special Educational Needs within lessons. Current guidance is given in *Safe Practice in Physical Education* (BAALPE 1995), which is used as a consultation document in cases of dispute in common law (see p. 21 'Physical Education and the Law').

The advice on supervision of pupils states:

> **Teachers should know of any individual needs and strengths of pupils. A teacher's awareness of any special educational needs, disabilities or medical conditions of pupils has often been significant in cases of negligence considered by the courts.**
>
> (p. 38d)

> Special safety precautions in determining the appropriate nature and level of an activity will be necessary when a pupil is inexperienced, immature, has a disability or demonstrates behavioural disorder.
>
> (p. 38f)

All teachers should read Chapter 8. Particular reference should be made to the section on prior considerations on p. 77 which includes:

> **Teachers in charge of a pupil with special educational needs must:**
>
> a. **know the nature of a child's learning problem, disability, emotional or behavioural disorder;**
>
> b. **be aware of any constraints on physical activities as a result of the disability or the regime of medication.**

Be prepared for difficulties which may be experienced (p. 77, 8.4.2), e.g.

- poor coordination
- lack of spatial concept or perception
- slow reaction time
- variable levels of concentration
- a short span of concentration
- cardiovascular inhibition
- muscle spasm
- sensory loss
- poor fine/gross motor skills.

Inclusion summary

The following (Sugden and Talbot 1996, p. 2) are reminders of the difficulties between access and opportunity. It is the latter which needs addressing. The focus has shifted from the needs/requirements of individuals to the quality and appropriateness of provision.

Access	Opportunity
• removing constraints, barriers	• making possible, relevant
• allowing in	• facilitating participation, enablement
• opening up	• welcoming in and including
• adding to existing provision	• adapting existing provision, making suitable
• patronage	• partnership
• equal access	• equity within programmes

Chapter 3

Motor Skill Development – Pinpointing the Difficulties

Having looked at the relevant documents which state legal and desired requirements in relation to PE, it will now be necessary to identify individual needs. To help consider the process a task analysis is given to help readers break down skills so as to provide tasks more appropriately matched to individual needs. The aim is to pinpoint the underlying problem. Is it one of motor ability (physical skills), lack of understanding (planning) or are there other reasons?

Remember that behavioural problems are so often the result of frustration through being unable to do the task/activity being presented.

As highlighted in paragraph 5 of the statements from the National Curriculum (DES 1991) on p. 13, there are many pupils whose Special Educational Needs in relation to Physical Education are often overlooked. Teachers need to be aware of behaviour which may indicate movement difficulties and associated problems.

Pupils may have difficulty with:

- sequencing of action/ideas

- responding to tasks through lack of either motor ability or understanding

- rhythmical movement patterns with many associated problems

- decision making

- planning movements

- predicting what is going to happen next

- transferring skills learnt in one situation to another

- personal organisation, especially with clothing and equipment

- movements requiring strength, endurance and flexibility.

Many pupils will have a poor self concept which will affect overall performance.

Task analysis

Two tasks have been selected for the purpose:

- **an everyday task (going to a table , sitting down to pour oneself a drink)**

- **a task related to Physical Education (games – sending and receiving with a bat and ball)**

The analysis considers the **physical demands** in terms of **movement skills** and **cognitive demands** in terms of **planning** and **understanding.**
In all tasks we have to consider:

1. the skills of the person performing the task

2. the environment in which it is being performed, e.g. Is everything still and constant or is it changing through interaction with others? Is equipment moving?

It is recommended that readers attempt these two tasks in order to familiarise themselves with activities which for the most part are taken for granted as being easy to perform. The aim is to make readers consider the demands made on those children whose development may not be refined sufficiently to perform the tasks effectively. By considering how many sub-skills are required within each of the tasks, it is hoped that readers will have a better insight as to where and at what stage problems may occur. For example, if a child has difficulty with maintaining balance they will have further difficulties in performing tasks which require each hand to undertake a different activity simultaneously (holding a beaker and pouring).

The purpose of these tasks is to improve readers' powers of observation.

Following a demonstration observers are invited to make a list of all the sub-skills needed in order to make the process successful. The authors have identified some skills, but there may be additional ones which readers might add.

Worksheet – Task 1

A functional activity

A typical lunch time activity in a primary school: going to a table, sitting down to pour oneself a drink from a jug into a beaker.

Equipment

Provide a jug containing water, a beaker and a table and chair of appropriate height.

Instructions

Go to the table.
Pull back the chair.
Sit on the chair.
Reach for the jug and pour a beaker of water and drink it.

Question

What skills does the performer need to make the task successful? Identify and name as many sub-skills as you can within the task being performed (e.g. ability to walk, ability to look).

Task 1

Analysis of physical and cognitive demands with some suggested responses from those with differing kinds of special need

Key to titles:
Developmental Coordination Disorder   DCD
Emotional and behavioural difficulties   EBD
Hearing impairment   Hearing
Learning difficulties   Learning
Physical difficulties   Physical
Visual impairment   Visual
✓ Depending on severity
❖ Maybe
Blank suggests no problems
(*Note:* In this example pupils with hearing difficulties are perceived as having no other problem, but rarely will this be the case.)

Physical demands	DCD	EBD	Hearing	Learning	Physical	Visual
Ability to stand still	❖	❖		❖	❖	
Ability to look, to focus, to see everything within the field of vision	❖	❖		❖		✓
Ability to recognise designated destinations, i.e. their table, their chair	❖	❖		❖		✓
Ability to walk forwards		❖		✓	❖	
Ability to stop at the appropriate place – this involves making decisions and judgements about distance from the table	✓	❖		✓	❖	✓
Ability to bend forward to pick up the chair with one or two hands – this requires knowledge of weight of the chair, ability to lean forward leaving enough space allowing the chair to be lifted upwards and backwards without landing on own feet	✓	❖		✓	❖	✓
Ability to lower body weight, to bend knees to the appropriate level, to grasp chair, pull chair sufficiently forward and lower body weight, gently to sit on chair surface as this is now unseen. What are you relying on: memory? Past experience? (All to do with body awareness/ body schema cognition)	✓	❖		✓	✓	
Ability to balance and control movement (applying appropriate body tension as and where needed)	✓	✓		❖	✓	

Physical demands	DCD	EBD	Hearing	Learning	Physical	Visual
Ability to use appropriate grip, strength and timing in pulling the chair in underneath the knees	✓			◆	✓	
Ability to know when to stop pulling the chair		◆		◆		
Ability to reach and grasp the beaker, maintaining the beaker still whilst reaching and grasping the jug which is a different sized grasp	✓	◆		◆	✓	✓
Ability to place the jug down on the table with the appropriate amount of force so as not to create a noise or spillage	◆	◆		◆	◆	◆
Ability to lift the beaker hand to find the mouth, tilt the beaker at the appropriate angle to get the right amount of liquid	◆			◆	◆	
Ability to breathe at the appropriate time, i.e. breathe, sip and swallow	◆			◆	◆	
Ability to place the beaker down on the table with the appropriate amount of force	◆	◆		◆	◆	
Ability to plan the necessary moves	✓	✓		✓	◆	✓
Knowing that the chair needs to be moved away from the table				✓		
Knowing that enough space needs to be created for the body to fit into the space	✓	◆		✓	◆	✓
Selecting the correct movement pathway		◆		◆		✓
Manoeuvring in the space created between the table and the chair, which involves judgement of space created and also knowledge of one's body shape and size	✓	✓		✓	✓	✓
Making decisions about whether or not to turn the spout around if it is not facing the right way	✓	◆		✓	◆	✓
Recognising that the jug needs to be lifted higher than the beaker, i.e. knowing that water is a liquid and has to flow downwards	◆	◆		✓	✓	✓
Being aware of alignment, i.e. moving objects towards each other with the jug higher than the beaker (still gripping, tilt the wrist at the right angle so that water goes into the beaker with the appropriate amount of force)	✓	◆		✓	✓	◆
Watching and judging where to stop	✓	◆		✓	✓	✓

Worksheet – Task 2

A practical activity appropriate for Key Stages 1 and 2, which is a task requiring cooperation with a partner

Sending and receiving activity using a bat and a ball and working with a partner (both standing still).

Equipment

Provide a basket containing different sized bats and balls. Invite two people to come and perform the task, preferably people not used to working together.

Instructions

Select a bat and ball between you.
Send, hit back, receive and repeat.
Have five goes on each role and then change over.

Extra task

See how many times you can do this within one minute.
Does this make a difference to your success rate?

Question

What skills do performers have which make this cooperative task successful?

Questions to aid discussion and observation

- What method of sending did you use?
- How could you make the task harder?
- How could you simplify the task?
- Were you happy with the equipment?
- What distance between you gave you success in the task?
- Was the bat ready as a target to be hit?
- Where did the partner hold the bat: at the side, high or low ?
- What role does previous experience play in the process?
- Does skill level affect the outcome?
- Were there any adjustments made by either player in either role?
- Did the participants seem happy with their choice of equipment?
- Which of the tasks did you find the easiest?

Task 2

Analysis of physical, cognitive and social demands of both participants

Key to titles:
Developmental Coordination Disorder DCD
Emotional and behavioural difficulties EBD
Hearing impairment Hearing
Learning difficulties Learning
Physical difficulties Physical
Visual impairment Visual
✓ Depending on severity
❖ Maybe
Blank suggests no problems

Joint planning ability – working with others	DCD	EBD	Hearing	Learning	Physical	Visual
Ability to listen to the task requirement	❖	❖	✓			
Ability to understand the task	❖	❖		✓		
Ability to make choices and select appropriate equipment	❖	✓		✓	❖	✓
Ability to communicate		✓	❖	✓		❖
Ability to decide on roles (this may or may not involve talking)	❖	✓		✓		❖
Ability to select the size of the area in which to perform the task	✓	✓		✓	❖	✓
Ability to establish where each person will stand to start the task	❖	✓		✓	❖	❖
Willingness to meet the challenge of the task	❖	❖	❖	✓	❖	❖
Willingness to meet partner's needs	✓		❖		✓	✓

Some suggested identified skills

Sender: physical demands	DCD	EBD	Hearing	Learning	Physical	Visual
Ability to stand and have a stable base	✓	❖			✓	
Ability to transfer weight from back to front foot	✓	❖		✓	✓	
Ability to release the ball at the right time and to the correct place	❖	❖		✓	❖	✓
Ability to watch the flight of the ball onto the bat	✓			❖	❖	✓

Sender: physical demands	DCD	EBD	Hearing	Learning	Physical	Visual
Ability to curve fingers around the ball and bend arms towards the body when receiving the ball back from batter	✓	◆		◆	✓	✓
Ability to move to receive ball if necessary	✓			✓	✓	✓

Sender: planning	DCD	EBD	Hearing	Learning	Physical	Visual
Ability to judge the appropriate moment to send the ball	✓	✓		✓	✓	✓
Ability to judge where to send the ball and at what force and speed	✓	✓		✓	✓	✓
Ability to prepare to receive the ball back	✓			✓	✓	✓
Ability to allow the hands to give as the ball is received so that the force is absorbed	✓	✓		✓	✓	✓

Batter: physical demands	DCD	EBD	Hearing	Learning	Physical	Visual
Ability to stand and have a stable base	✓	◆			✓	
Ability to look at sender	✓				✓	✓
Ability to track (watch) the ball from sender's hands	✓	✓		✓	✓	✓
Ability to receive (see? feel?) the ball on the bat	✓	✓		✓	◆	✓
Ability to react and adjust body tension in order to send ball back to partner	✓	✓		✓	◆	✓
Ability to organise body weight from back foot, sideways stance, with forward momentum transferred through the whole body	✓	✓		✓	✓	✓
Ability to watch the flight of the ball back to partner	◆	◆		◆	◆	✓
Ability to change role from receiving to sending	◆	✓		✓		

Batter: planning	DCD	EBD	Hearing	Learning	Physical	Visual
Ability to judge where and when the ball will arrive	✓	◆		✓		✓
Ability to watch the ball from the sender's hand and judge the speed and pathway of the ball	✓	◆		◆	◆	✓
Ability to anticipate the moment of impact	✓	◆		✓	✓	✓
Ability to adjust the angle of the bat	✓	✓		✓	✓	✓

Difficulties encountered by pupils with impairments

The tasks relating to functional skills and bat and ball skills (Task 1 and Task 2) will have heightened awareness of difficulties which children with various forms of impairment may experience when performing the two tasks. **The following list summarises difficulties which may be experienced by pupils with varying forms of impairment in a variety of tasks, both functional skills within the classroom and those related to Physical Education. Such limitations must be borne in mind when planning activities and delivering the Programmes of Study .**

- *Physical:* posture, mobility, safety, balance, control, manual skills, spatial awareness (especially body judgement), access to buildings, involuntary movements, slow reactions, lack of strength.

- *Sensory:* balance, safety, communication (visually impaired children may have difficulty in gaining enough information to fulfil tasks).

- *Learning:* communication, understanding, remembering, safety, working with others, planning, decision making, lower level and rate of learning, difficulties in transforming information from one situation to another.

- *Behavioural:* inability to stay on task, non-conforming, inability to work with others, safety, communication, lack of confidence, lack of skills, lack of self control, feeling threatened by the environment, adjusting to different situations, learning difficulties, difficulty with coping with open-ended tasks.

- *Coordination*: lack of skill, lack of coordination, speech difficulties, lack of experience, concentration, frustration, slower reactions, lack of planning ability

Principles of progression

The following are the general principles of progression when planning and delivering Programmes of Study for children. Pupils generally move from:

- dependence to independence in learning;

- performing given tasks to being able to structure their own;

- using given criteria to judge others' performance, to developing their own criteria to evaluate their own and others' performance;

- simple tasks to more complex and difficult ones;

- natural (developmental) movements to skilful/artistic/technical or aesthetic performance;

- developing movement patterns to learning conventional skills and sequences of movement.

(Sugden and Talbot 1996, p. 4)

Remember that some children with Special Educational Needs will require

- **more time**
- **structured tasks**
- **simpler activities in order to have access to Programmes of Study.**

Key factors in analysing movement skill development

All actions are made up of a sequence of discrete skills: 'A movement skill is an organised sequence of movement directed towards a desired outcome.' (Sugden and Keogh 1990)

A useful framework for considering movement skill development was presented by Sugden and Keogh in 1985 and has been adapted here.

- **Postural control:** Children need a *stable shoulder girdle* and a *stable pelvic girdle* in order to be able to isolate arm, leg and head movements either together, individually or in isolation.

- **Planning ability:** children need to be able to *organise* their movements, develop spatial awareness, *plan* pathways, sequence and vary the rhythm of their actions. They need to be able to *select*, *order* and *adjust* their responses in relation to task requirements. They also need to *repeat* and *practice* skills in order to *refine* their movements.

- **Control of force:** children need to be able to *judge* how much muscle strength is required in a range of tasks in a variety of situations.

- **Manipulation control, reach and grasp (fine motor skills):** children need to develop the ability to *control* movements of the hands in order to manipulate them in a manner appropriate to the task, e.g. propulsion in swimming, gesture in dance, grip in gymnastic activities, receiving and sending objects in athletic activities and games.

See pp. 38–40 for activities to help improve each of these areas for children at Key Stages 1 and 2.

Making tasks accessible through a progressional model

Opposite is a useful model for analysing movement demands of individuals within certain situations. The boxes can be seen as progressional. Children experiencing difficulties in Box 1 will find the demands of Box 4 very daunting. It is therefore recommended that having identified physical and cognitive needs through a variety of tasks, children should be taught activities relating to Box 1 first. This will enable the children to experience success .

The following pages use this model of the four boxes to relate activities to the National Curriculum Programmes of Study. These boxes also take individual children through the progressional stages.

- **Stage 1/Box 1** starts with the child performing activities from a stationary base whether it be sitting, standing or lying.

- **Stage 2/Box 2** provides activities for the child moving within an area that is stable/stationary. Hence the importance of providing individual bases which the children can move away from and return to.

- **Stage 3/Box 3** provides opportunities for the child who is working from a stationary base but apparatus/equipment is moving, e.g. a turning rope, a ball bouncing to be caught.

- **Stage 4/Box 4** has the child moving freely within an area whilst everybody else is doing the same. The variables, e.g. making decisions, changing directions and taking avoiding action, are very demanding.

We know from research by Sugden and Keogh (1990) that children with a variety of special educational needs will have performance inadequacies and lack consistency when performing tasks. They need longer to perform or execute movements and are slower in reacting to tasks and intercepting or avoiding objects.

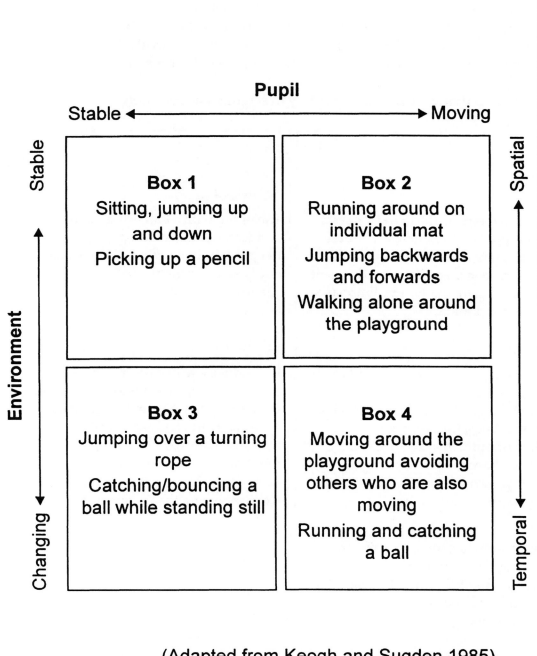

Different types of movement in relation to environmental conditions

Pupil

Stable ◄————————————► Moving

Stable

Spatial

Environment

Box 1

Sitting, jumping up and down

Picking up a pencil

Box 2

Running around on individual mat

Jumping backwards and forwards

Walking alone around the playground

Box 3

Jumping over a turning rope

Catching/bouncing a ball while standing still

Box 4

Moving around the playground avoiding others who are also moving

Running and catching a ball

Changing

Temporal

(Adapted from Keogh and Sugden 1985)

Programme of study

Games

Pupils stationary
Some games activities which can be planned and performed with pupils remaining on or close to their own base.

Pupils moving
Some games activities which can be planned and performed with pupils moving away from a base and back.

Examples of activities to improve accuracy in sending and receiving

Box 1	Box 2
Key Stage 1	*Key Stage 1*
Place small targets (bean bags, quoits, shapes) on the floor and ask children to hit the targets as hard as possible by throwing bean bags. Try from different positions. Changing hands. Emphasise accuracy and force.	Travelling with a ball using hands and feet. Rolling, chasing, stopping. Keeping the ball within a prescribed boundary. Aiming the ball at different shapes and at targets at different levels.
Key Stage 2	*Key Stage 2*
Individually bouncing a ball and catching, on the spot. Prior to this teach these skills to allow children access, use hoops, shapes, mats as targets. Use a variety of different sized balls using one/two hands. Give challenges: ' Try to beat your own record'. 'How many can you do in a given time?'	Individually with a ball perform a pattern of actions, e.g. moving around the base – 4 bounces with right hand, 4 bounces with left hand, 2 pats upwards with right hand, 2 pats upwards with left hand, catch and carry the ball to touch it down on a line. Keep repeating the pattern.
Using alternate hands, combining bouncing and hitting in the air. Vary the force used to bounce the ball. Attempt continuous bouncing whilst travelling.	

Pupils stationary

Some games activities which can be planned and performed with pupils remaining on or close to their own base.

Pupils moving

Some games activities which can be planned and performed with pupils moving away from a base and back.

Examples of activities to improve accuracy in sending and receiving

Box 3	Box 4
Key Stage 1	*Key Stage 1*
In pairs near a designated base, each has a different role. **A** runs to target and back to score. **B** aims ball/bean bag into target to count how many in one minute. Change roles.	In pairs, one ball per pair, send the ball backwards and forwards to each other, rolling/bouncing, using hands/feet. Moving freely within a defined area.
Key Stage 2	*Key Stage 2*
In pairs, one ball per pair. **A** aims the ball at a target, **B** retrieves and rolls it back to sender. Have 3 goes and change roles. How many in time given?	**Ball tag** Two catchers with a ball each within a defined area.
	Children run in general space. Children with ball attempt to tag runners. When tagged, ball is transferred to tagged person who receives the ball. Alternatively when tagged, child collects another ball from the appropriate basket and becomes an additional catcher. Who is the last person to be caught?
	A small sided game – size to vary according to needs already assessed.

Programme of study

Gymnastic activities

Pupils stationary
Some gymnastic activities which can be planned and performed with pupils remaining on or close to their own base.

Pupils moving
Some gymnastic activities which can be planned and performed with pupils moving away from a base and back.

Examples of activities to improve travelling skills

Box 1	Box 2
Key Stage 1 On teacher cue, move and stop, e.g. 'Travel–stop', 'Run–stop'. Run on the the spot, balance on a body part, e.g. balance on tummies only.	*Key Stage 1* Travelling on hands and feet, or on feet plus other body parts, turning, rolling, jumping away from, towards, over and around a base (e.g. mat, shape) or designated area. Travelling actions with changes of direction going from and returning to, off, on, around – changes of direction. Travelling over, under, around through apparatus. 'Run around mat once, sit on your mat.' (This requires memory and recall, remembering where the sequence started; it also involves planning ability.)

Examples of activities to improve jumping skills

Box 1	Box 2
Key Stage 2 Using an individual base, practise a range of jumping activities on or near the base. Vary body shape in air and take off from one or two feet.	*Key Stage 2* Jumping pattern combination, e.g. jump, jump, hop along mat/base, turn, repeat. Vary pattern, vary direction/ speed.

Pupils stationary
Some gymnastic activities which can
be planned and performed with pupils
remaining on or close to their own base.

Pupils moving
Some gymnastic activities which can
be planned and performed with pupils
moving away from a base and back.

Examples of activities to improve travelling and balancing

Box 3	Box 4
Key Stage 1 Travel away from/around your base, return and show a balanced shape on your base. Can you repeat this? What is the pathway you are using?	*Key Stage 1* Travelling with different actions freely within the room, return to base on teacher cue and show a balanced shape. Repeat. Can you find your own base? Using apparatus: travel around apparatus arrangement, find different places to be still and balanced. Encourage children to find different starting positions. Everyone working at the same time.

Examples of activities to improve travelling and jumping skills

Box 3	Box 4
Key Stage 2 Working with a partner – taking turns, e.g. **A** does 3 jumps. **B** does 3 jumps – keep the pattern going. **A** makes a wide bridge shape with weight on hands and feet. **B** travels through spaces created by the shape. Change roles. **A** performs a roll across the mat. **B** does the same (take turns). **A** is stationary until **B** completes the action.	*Key Stage 2* With a partner, combine a jumping pattern – one leading, the other following. Move freely around hall varying directions and speed whilst avoiding others. Change leader. Using a range of apparatus, follow partner's jumping pattern (around, over, etc.) whilst avoiding other couples working at the same time. Add an asymmetrical balance at an appropriate place.

Programme of study

Dance

Pupils stationary
Some dance ideas which can be created and performed with pupils remaining on or close to their own base.

Pupils moving
Some dance ideas which can be created and performed with pupils moving away and back to place.

Examples of activities to develop expressive qualities in hand and foot gestures

Box 1

Key Stage 1

Hand patterns
(focus on hands, eyes to follow movement – this helps concentration) Sitting in place, begin by exploring gestures – aerial pathways. Start close to the body, reach out, extend and return to centre. Develop with contrast in speeds.

Key Stage 2

Foot patterns, e.g. sporting activities theme
(focus on feet, gesture and stillness) Children explore a variety of stepping patterns associated with different footwear – wellies, skates, football boots, ballet shoes, roller blades, boxing shoes, tennis shoes.

Box 2

Key Stage 1

Travelling steps with hands leading to make patterns and simple motifs, varying levels, including twists, turns and jumps. Encourage clarity of shape in hand movement and expressive qualities to symbolise intention of the gesture, e.g. anger, greeting, conflict.

Key Stage 2

Compose a simple motif involving travelling, stillness and turning.

Jump – within a confined area (involving counting the steps to move into turning/jump to stillness). Music could be inhibiting since pace will be dependent on character selected.

Pupils stationary
Some dance ideas which can be created and performed with pupils remaining on or close to their own base.

Pupils moving
Some dance ideas which can be created and performed with pupils moving away and back to place.

Examples of activities to develop expressive qualities in hand and foot gestures

Box 3	Box 4
Key Stage 1	*Key Stage 1*
Hand patterns In pairs, **A** performs hand gestures, **B** responds – using action/reaction in gesture.	**Foot patterns** In pairs, **A** and **B** create a similar pose (according to the theme) and travel away from each other and back to place copying the foot pattern and expressive quality, e.g. skater hold starting position – slide, slide, twirl and glide.
Group activity In small groups, hold hands and pass on a squeeze. Develop by varying the gesture – and repeating in canon in a group dance.	
Key Stage 2	*Key Stage 2*
In pairs, create a simple motif starting with a pose symbolising a sporting action, travel away, add a jumping action. Finish in the original pose.	Dance framework: for a dance based on a sporting theme. Children work in pairs, select a sporting theme as the stimulus and create a simple dance. Hold starting position, travel, turn or jump to end in appropriate pose. Emphasise variety of pathways, directions and levels.

Assessment – looking at motor skills and associated activities

Key Stage 1

Postural control	Ability to stop Running action Sitting/kneeling Stand to sit/lie Symmetrical bases including hands and knees Muscle tone Fitness Balance
Planning ability	Body awareness Spatial awareness Identifying correct body parts with eyes closed Tracking an object • crossing the midline of the body • following a moving object away from the body/ coming towards the body at different levels Reactions – throw a bean bag in the air, clap and catch bean bag Ability to concentrate – watch/listen
Control of force	Aiming – hitting a variety of targets Throwing, rolling, bouncing – varying the amount of force needed to control objects Following and trapping a ball
Manual ability	Reaching for objects with weight on different bases Kneeling, using hands and fingers to make a ball go around the body Looking at hand dominance Grasping and carrying different-sized objects Bouncing and catching Using quoits as bats
Cooperation/communication	Taking turns – watching Discussing Listening Making decisions
Number concepts	Jump and count at the same time Aim/hit a target, count how many times

Assessment – looking at motor skills and associated activities

Key Stage 2

Postural control

Ability to stop – showing correct stance and body tension
Running action – on the spot, moving, adding another action
Maintaining good posture whilst performing a variety of actions, e.g. jump, hop – vary directions
Actions whilst using different bases, e.g. bunny jumps, weight on hands and knees
Ability to maintain posture whilst doing a sequence of actions
Muscle tone
Fitness
Balance

Planning ability

Body awareness – relationship of different parts to each other (eyes closed)
Spatial awareness – speed of moving self and objects in relation to space and others
Tracking objects
• crossing the midline of the body
• travelling with an object, keeping it under control through a variety of spaces/people
Reactions
• throw a ball in the air, clap and catch
• stationary/ moving
Memory
• ability to recall and demonstrate a series of actions in the correct order
• presented visually/orally
Ability to concentrate – watch/listen

Control of force

Aiming – hitting a variety of targets at different levels
Throwing, rolling, bouncing, varying the amount of force needed to control objects
Sending and receiving objects from others, varying speed and direction as appropriate

Manual ability	Reaching for objects with weight on different bases
	Kneeling, using hands and fingers to make a ball go around the body
	Looking at hand dominance
	Grasping and propelling a variety of different-sized objects
	Bat and ball skills – on own (making sequences), with others
Cooperation/communication	Taking turns – watching
	Discussing
	Listening
	Making decisions
	Working with a variety of partners
Pattern and sequencing	Ability to keep rhythm and momentum, with and without equipment, working in twos.

Chapter 4

Stepping Stones to Enable Children to have Access to National Curriculum Physical Education

Core skills – what are these?

As already stressed the key to access for children with Special Educational Needs is matching the tasks to the learner's needs.

What are these needs? First, consider physical needs, i.e. core physical skills.

Travelling/moving

Running, jumping, hopping, skipping, with changes of direction and speed.

Rolling – contrast of extension with curl

1. Can children get full extension when doing one complete sideways roll? Arms and legs should remain stretched throughout.

2. Can children remain curled with head tucked in when doing a curled roll? If not, are they lacking in strength in the pelvic or shoulder region?

Forward and backward rolls are skills in their own right and teachers must satisfy themselves that the prerequisite requirements are taught prior to teaching these activities.

Balance

1. *Static*. These activities are important and attention should be paid to the correct posture for each activity, encouraging children to 'feel' correct positions. Balancing on stable bases and being still with correct posture is important. Sitting, standing, lying, balancing on hands and knees are all symmetrical bases which

children need to practise. Can children feel they are straight? Head position for each is important. Where do the eyes look?

2. *Dynamic.* Balancing whilst walking, running, jumping, hopping, climbing and swinging involves maintaining correct posture whilst moving. Children with poor coordination will have difficulties with these activities. Again, using different bases, e.g. kneeling, sitting, lying, is also important.

Body awareness

It is important that children develop an ability to do things without sight. Check that children are able to maintain balance once sight has been removed.

Weight on hands

Strength in the shoulder girdle is needed to perform this skill efficiently. Lack of upper body strength will:

- affect games skills (control of force and effort)
- affect writing skills (fine motor control).

A stable upper body, i.e. good posture, is needed prior to getting hands and arms to do discrete movements, either together (weight on hands) or separately (throwing a ball with one hand to make contact with a bat held in the other hand).

Spatial ability

Children need to appreciate the relationship of objects to each other and how their bodies relate to those objects. The ability to move and manoeuvre successfully through a crowded classroom or avoid others whilst sending and receiving with balls in games lessons is vital. The more variables there are the more difficulty children will have in managing their bodies whilst making quick decisions about where to move next. For children with Special Educational Needs large games situations therefore can create major problems, as do cluttered classrooms with many objects to negotiate.

Pattern and sequencing

The ability to perform tasks rhythmically with fluidity often distinguishes the coordinated child from the uncoordinated child.

Sequencing of movements forms an important part of the Physical Education curriculum at Key Stages 1 and 2. Performing actions in a sequence which can be repeated accurately several times will enhance a child's learning ability, especially memory, concentration and motivation. Asking children to repeat actions which have to be copied or require instructions to be followed will allow them to develop skills of concentration and memory, as well as improving and refining physical skills.

Object manipulation – ball skills working with a partner

Children need to be able to work alone in their own space or with their piece of equipment prior to being asked to work with a partner (see Chapter 5). Some children are socially isolated and find working with others difficult. This is an area that needs to be planned and progressively developed.

Why children may not conform

If children fail to hear, see, or understand what is required the lessons become meaningless to them. This can often result in children misbehaving.

So far the focus has been on lack of physical ability, i.e. movement skills, but *not communicating* the correct information can also result in misbehaviour. Remember:

- Inappropriate behaviour is a Special Educational Need in its own right and needs to be dealt with appropriately.

- Behavioural problems should not be seen in isolation but are always related to the situation at a particular time.

- When teaching Physical Education the teacher has control of the context in which the children are working.

There follow examples of situations/scenarios which might arise prior to or within the Physical Education lesson. Some possible causes are suggested, with courses of action to avoid similar situations. Many problems arise when children are unable to cope with the task/environment in which they find themselves, i.e. they have a Special Need in Physical Education.

Children whose behaviour does not conform to expectations

Prior to lessons

What you see	Could it be?	Possible courses of action
• Absenteeism • Regular excuse notes	• Fear • Sense of failing • Hiding signs of child abuse	• Talk to/share concerns with other teachers • Investigate patterns of absenteeism • Communicate concerns to senior management
• Forgetting kit	• All of the above • Skin complaints • Onset of puberty • Inappropriate clothing • Lack of dressing skills • Problems with sequencing – not getting things in the right order	• Communication within school • Alternative changing arrangements • Appropriate clothing • Provide a dressing and undressing routine as part of an individual programme
• Inability to stay on task whilst getting changed for PE	• Too many distractions • Lack of skill • Lack of organisation • Lack of concentration	• If necessary, extra supervision for children needing help with dressing and undressing • Change the venue to where there are fewer distractions • Establish a procedure for changing within a designated area – this needs careful consideration regarding privacy, space and obstacles/ equipment which may cause distraction
• Children making fun of or ridiculing others; overt comments about children's 'non-conforming' appearance, e.g. the overweight child, the tall, the thin, the unclean child	• Lack of sensitivity to children's appearance, physique • Inappropriate clothing	• Teachers need to be sensitive to such issues • Open discussion about appearance and feelings • More responsibility and trust encouraged through the curriculum • Relate to healthy exercise, for obese children. Link with health-related activities. • Consider altering changing arrangements for PE

During lessons

What you see	Could it be?	Possible courses of action
• The child who tears around, touches the equipment, generally does not listen or respond • Children who shout and make noises	• Children have difficulty in adapting their behaviour to different environments, particularly open space, freedom and choice • Children have not understood the task • They may not have heard • They many not know how to stop on signal • A cry for help	• Prior to the lesson make sure that boundaries are established and that the children know procedures and rules, e.g. where to go at the start of lessons and what to do once there. Children need to have a structured, active task (not 'go and sit still') • Give children a base from which to work perhaps a more confined space, e.g. 'go to the red mat or yellow hoop' • Setting a task where the majority of the children are going to conform – you are then free to observe
• Refusal to work with others	• Fear of being rejected • Unfamiliarity with working with a variety of partners	• Make it accepted procedure that partners/groups change at regular intervals so that all children work with a variety of others
• Refusal to take part in certain parts of the lesson	• Too many variables within the game/activity • Skill level of the task too difficult	• Simplify activities, only small sided games • Making sure that the skills are progressional and that tasks are matched to learners' needs • Making action in dance dramatic, with strong body tension if appropriate
• Does not listen to instructions/starts activity before told. • Does not watch/does not look. • Easily side-tracked	• Poor hearing • Difficulties in processing information • Inability to select relevant material from background information (lack of auditory/visual discrimination) • Too many words, speech too rapid, monotonous tone, too many background noises	• Use a multi-sensory approach to giving information • Repeat instructions • Allow time for children to question if they have not got all the relevant information or do not understand • Give clear, concise instructions

What you see	Could it be?	Possible courses of action
• Social isolation	• Lack of social skills • Poor hygiene	• Work with an adult • Groupings should be variable and flexible • Working on an individual programme • Communication with senior management
• Inappropriate fulfilling of the task	• Insufficient information to fulfil the task	• Careful use of language and demonstration
• A child breaking the rules and cheating	• Aims and objectives are not made clear to the children • Inability to understand or follow the rules • Wanting to win without effort; more interested in the end result rather than the process • The teacher is inconsistent in rewarding and admonishing	• There should be a well established shared awards and punishments system • Make sure that you give all children enough to concentrate on so that they are not concerned with the behaviour of others • Rules that are negotiated and explained, rather than imposed
• Disruptive behaviour	• Failure to allow children enough time to plan or evaluate • Inner frustration caused by boredom, etc. • Boredom – task too easy, too difficult	• Give children more responsibility – sharing in the planning and evaluating • Opportunity to talk through the task • Look at the statement of need and identify behaviours which may present safety difficulties within the Physical Education context • If disruptive behaviour is affecting themselves or others within the lesson and is likely to cause accidents, the children involved should be excluded and help and advice sought from senior management
• Physical violence	• No opportunity to discuss • The child does not feel valued. • Lack of self control	• Establish whether this is occurring in other lessons; if so, after discussion, see whether individual targets can be set to help with behaviour modification

What you see	Could it be?	Possible courses of action
• Atypical behaviour – e.g. aggressive, apathetic behaviour	• Trauma at home • Not feeling well • Fallen out with friends	• Try to get to the underlying cause through discussion with others
• Children who switch off/lack concentration	• The lesson is too long • The pace is inappropriate • The content is too complex • Lack of challenge	• Discuss with PE coordinator • Keep children active and involved; give responsibility for own actions when working with others • Address the issue of differentiation, making sure that the task can be simplified if necessary or be made more challenging for those who need it.
• Listless children	• Lack of sleep • Lack of food • Inappropriate clothing • Poor level of fitness	• Link health education programme with health-related exercise in the Physical Education programme
• The 'class idiot' – deliberately messing about and doing things wrongly	• A cover up for inability • Negative reinforcement by the teacher and other classmates	• Try to deal with the situation without an audience • Make sure you have an activity in which the rest of the class are busy so that you are free to deal with the issue. Avoid confrontation or ridicule situations if possible • Patterns of behaviour need to be changed, maybe with support from others
• Slow to respond to instructions	• Lack of understanding • Poor at seeing/interpreting information. • Poor at hearing/interpreting information	• Make sure instructions are always repeated • If visually presented, reinforce with auditory cues and vice versa • If necessary use manual manipulation – this needs to be used sensitively and appropriately

Having recognised some problem areas, here are some aspects that need to be addressed. Consider:

- physical ability level;

- level of understanding – often misbehaviour results from inappropriate tasks, being unable to cope with the open-ended situations, the larger environment and the less rigid structure;

- failure to allow children time to plan, to evaluate and to question.

Sometimes children are naughty to gain attention so that they will be excluded from certain activities. Could this be a cry for help?

Remember that the largest group of children with Special Educational Needs are those with Moderate Learning Difficulties. These children will have difficulty in processing information. Many have coordination and perceptual difficulties which need to be considered. As in reading , the skills that are lacking need to be taught – for example, the ability to look at something/someone is a skill in its own right, as is the ability to sit and to stand still.

The key to success for all children with Special Educational Needs is matching the tasks to learners' needs. Hopefully we have highlighted some of the behaviours you will see, suggested some of the causes and provided some strategies for helping improve class management situations and children's individual skills.

The need for support

In some instances it is not possible for the teacher to deal appropriately with all kinds of difficulties without support from another individual. This should be provided where and when deemed appropriate, as is the practice within the classroom for academic subjects. Hence the importance of collecting relevant evidence of need in Physical Education.

Regarding support, teachers need to ask themselves **Why? When? Where?** The Code of Practice should be used to identify difficulties at the appropriate stages.

Stage 1

The teacher of Physical Education, with the aid of the SENCO, needs to think about class management in order to make the Physical Education lessons accessible to children with Special Educational Needs. This could involve:

- making instructions/demonstrations clearer, simpler or more specific;
- making tasks simpler (e.g. see Breaking down ball skills (p. 88) and Differentiation (p. 57));
- enabling children to choose with whom they work;
- adjusting expectations.

Stage 2

For children whose needs are not adequately met through Stage 1, the teacher needs to draw up, with the aid of the SENCO, an individual educational programme. This may include the use of some 'In-lesson' support, or where relevant some backup activities to enable these children to gain appropriate access to the Physical Education curriculum.

Stages 3, 4 and 5 involve further and outside help. For ideas/activities for Individual Educational Programmes see Chapter 6.

Teacher skills

> **Improving pupils' movement skills helps to change feelings of under-achievement, low self-esteem and disaffection.**

It can be very useful to have someone to observe and record pupils who have difficulties with some activities. The observer could be the headteacher, another class teacher, the SENCO, an ancillary helper, a governor or a parent. There follows a list of skills which teachers should have in order to meet appropriately the needs of individual pupils with SEN.

Summary of skills teachers need to provide appropriate programmes for pupils with Special Educational Needs

Observational skills
- what are we looking at?

Knowledge of
- the curriculum – PE and other areas which have relevance
- how the nature of pupils' impairments will affect learning potential and expectations
- pupils' interests, past experience, strengths/weaknesses
- medical conditions which may affect activities offered

Ability to
- match tasks to pupils' needs
- provide opportunities for pupils to plan, evaluate, work with others – use a range of teaching styles, e.g. teacher directed – children working on tasks with others independently, with appropriate guidance/interjections from the teacher
- analyse movements/break down tasks into smaller components
- manage time in relation to expectations – adjust time to meet expectations
- set realistic targets for pupils
- vary groupings according to task requirements
- record achievement within the school's assessment procedures
- communicate with the school's Special Educational Needs Coordinator
- where necessary, provide support staff with appropriate tasks for individual pupils within the class lesson

Consideration of
- social skills – the ability of pupils to work with others (adults, peers)

Remember the importance of the self concept

Chapter 5

Accessing the Curriculum for Children with Special Educational Needs

The diagram opposite suggests particular areas which need attention in order to provide access to the PE curriculum for children with Special Educational Needs.

All three aspects – **fitness, sequencing, partner work** – are often seen as stumbling blocks for children with special needs. Each one is dealt with separately and is related to National Curriculum requirements. The teacher needs to consider ways of **differentiating tasks** and readjusting outcomes for pupils with SEN.

Fitness

The General Requirements for Physical Education state:

> **To promote physical activity and healthy lifestyles, pupils should be taught:**
>
> - **to be physically active;**
>
> - **to adopt the best possible posture and the appropriate use of the body;**
>
> - **to engage in activities that develop cardiovascular health, flexibility, muscular strength and endurance.**

Physical activity

Children of all abilities should experience a range of physical activities and children with Special Educational Needs often need more physical activity in order to develop their delayed/deficient motor skills, which can be linked with poor flexibility, strength and stamina. For a variety of reasons these children are often reluctant to take part in physical activities in and beyond school, yet they are the ones who could benefit the most. The sense of well being and enhanced level of fitness resulting from regular and enjoyable physical activity can go a long way towards helping them develop a more positive self image.

Access to the Physical Education curriculum

To help children cope more effectively, focus on:

Fitness
Encouraging activity
Healthy lifestyles
Cardiovascular fitness
Strength – Posture
Flexibility

Sequencing
Timing
Patterning
Rhythm
Memory
Repetition

Partner work
Staying on task
Self discipline
Cooperating
Competing
Communicating

To help the teacher deliver more effectively, focus on:

Differentiation
Catering for the individual needs of children of all abilities
Matching tasks to learners' needs

Posture

Poor posture ←————→ Poor coordination

Ever since the 1933 Syllabus of Physical Training for Schools (Board of Education 1933), in which it was seen as central to the Physical Education curriculum, posture has rarely been mentioned in any document from central government. It is therefore heartening to see this aspect of education featured in the National Curriculum General Requirements for Physical Education.

However, as one of the purposes of Physical Education is to develop and manage the body, it is essential that through this area of the curriculum both teachers and children are made aware of the importance of good posture in their everyday lives. The analysis of functional skills (see p. 24) illustrates the importance of posture in performing simple skills. Within both Physical Education lessons and classroom activities good posture is absolutely essential. Teachers should encourage correct posture when children are standing, sitting, kneeling or lying.

An activity which assesses children's ability to be stable is to ask a child to balance on four points of the body, e.g. hands and knees, and then to stretch one hand forward and shake it in front of the body, moving the arm or wrist, while at the same time maintaining a stable base. Children with instability in the shoulder or pelvic girdle will lose balance and fall over, thus demonstrating an instability in this area which needs attention.

Lack of stability in the shoulder or pelvic girdle results in poor posture. Without strength and stability in these regions a child will exhibit poor coordination which will be particularly evident in games and gymnastic activities. **Themes in gymnastic activities which might help to develop strength in these areas are:**

- travelling on hands and feet
- travelling and balancing on different body parts.

Teaching safe jumping and steadiness in landings, encouraging children to bend the knees, allowing 'give' in the ankles and using arms to maintain balance can help to promote good posture in jumping activities.

From an early age children should be taught to understand the principles and simple techniques of adopting a suitable posture to lift and carry correctly, thus preventing injury to the lower back.

Cardiovascular health

Cardiovascular health refers to the efficient functioning of the circulatory and respiratory systems which is an aspect of fitness sometimes referred to as stamina. To develop and maintain cardiovascular health teachers need to ensure that children have plenty of opportunities to be physically active in lessons and at playtime.

Activities which involve large muscle groups such as brisk walking, skipping, jogging, running and chasing games, dancing, cycling and swimming will have a positive effect on children's cardiovascular health. The activities need to be enjoyable to engage children's interest and to help them increase the duration and intensity of the activity (see Bray 1993 for practical ideas).

Some children find open space and running and chasing games bewildering so, before setting children off to move freely in open space, set tasks involving vigorous activity 'in place', which for many children will create a more secure and structured environment. Tasks might be:

- jogging on the spot (use individual mats, markings to set boundaries)
- simple stepping/jumping patterns for a set period of time (music can be a motivator to help maintain interest in these activities).

Flexibility

Flexibility refers to mobility of the joints of the body. Children with Special Educational Needs should have opportunities to practise flexibility exercises with limbs moving in isolation and then together.

An activity which assesses children's flexibility is to stand with good posture, arms outstretched in front of the body, rotating both wrists in a circular movement, when rotating one wrist keep the rest of the body still. Inability to do this shows that there are lots of associated movements and instability in the shoulder girdle.

Muscular strength and endurance

Children need strength to maintain correct body posture for many task requirements. Children with Special Educational Needs often have poor muscle tone and in some cases will display a rather 'floppy' appearance.

For these children their lack of strength and endurance will be problematic in many aspects of Physical Education. There are implications for climbing on apparatus. It might be that some children should have an individual programme to enable them to develop this aspect of their fitness.

Sequencing

Planning and performing a sequence involves linking a series of identical or different actions whether the same or different with smooth transitions between the changes. Sequences will either take the form of a simple pattern with a clear beginning and end, or be more complex and ongoing with continuous repetition. Children should experience both. Activities should be made progressional.

Enabling children successfully to develop movement sequences

The following are examples of tasks which will allow the teacher to observe those children who may be off task and to identify those having difficulty interpreting the task. The first set of tasks involves performing simple actions directed by the teacher.

Sequencing Games Key Stage 1

- 'Run on your base until told to stop.'

- 'Perform continuous bouncy jumps on your base.' 'Stop!'

- 'Throw a bean bag in the air and catch it. Keep on repeating.'

- 'Send the bean bag away with three pushes with hands, feet or equipment and return to place with three pushes back.'

- 'Can you now plan and perform a pattern on your own?' (without teacher direction). In this task encourage the children to keep on repeating the pattern.

- 'In pairs, throwing and catching. Keep the rhythm/pattern going.'

Sequencing Games Key Stage 2

A prerequisite of this task is to make sure all children have been taught how to bounce a ball with one or two hands and are able to catch. It is also important that they are able to throw a ball upward with accuracy, e.g. to the top of their head, to a high target.

The task involves rhythm and patterning using balls. The aims are to

- develop upper body strength

- improve concentration

- keep to a constant rhythm to stay on task – the sound of the ball bouncing becomes a reinforcer

- improve memory

- increase motivation.

The task, which can be set either verbally or with a demonstration for children to copy, is:

Take a ball each, perform eight bounces using two hands simultaneously, four bounces using right hand, four bounces using left hand. Repeat, keeping the pattern going. Add to the complexity by

- repeating the above
- travelling around the base or linking with a partner.

Sequencing Gymnastic Activities Key Stage 1

Perform actions directed by teacher:

- 'Travel and stop.' 'Travel and change direction.'
- 'Travel and perform an action on the spot' (e.g. jumping).

Sequencing Gymnastic Activities Key Stage 2

This task involves combining/sequencing of foot patterns, e.g. 'Run, perform symmetrical jump in the air'. This involves running, stopping, taking off and landing on two feet with controlled landing, then repeating; it also involves the ability to negotiate space and make decisions.

Sequencing Dance Key Stage 1

- 'Travel on feet and stop' (stepping, skipping, sliding, hopping). Remember, skipping is a sequence of step, hop, step on opposite foot, hop. Children should be encouraged to step, hop, step, hop on the spot before they are expected to travel.
- 'March with knees high'. This encourages slowness in movement, marching requires them to put the whole foot down and the pattern is reinforced through the sound of feet meeting the floor. It is an activity which encourages an upright posture and is good for pelvic strength .

Sequencing Dance Key Stage 2

- 'Create a simple motif including stillness and travelling steps.' 'Repeat accurately.'
- 'Create a simple motif including leaping and turning into stillness.' 'Repeat accurately.'

Partner work

The General Requirements for Physical Education state that **to develop positive attitudes children should be taught:**

- to observe the conventions of fair play, honest competition and good sporting behaviour as individual participants, team members and spectators;
- how to cope with success and limitations in performance.

Children should have the opportunity to work with a variety of partners and the skill of the teacher is in adapting tasks to the different pairings of the children.

Helping children work successfully with partners

Children need opportunities to work on their own to practice activities individually prior to being asked to work with a partner. The following are examples of tasks or strategies which might be adopted.

Key Stage 1

- Watch your partner.

- Describe what you see, e.g. three balances plus one other activity. What is the other activity?

- Can you help your partner? Suggest ways to improve the performance. Criteria for assessment will need to have been discussed and shared beforehand.

- Find ways of combining aspects of each child's performance – this involves discussing, selecting, decision making , agreeing.

- Copy your partner's pattern – this may involve some reciprocal teaching, helping each other to improve.

- Combine ideas to create a more complex sequence.

- Adjust the work to make it more interesting (develop spatial or dynamic qualities), through games, gymnastic activities or dance.

Key Stage 2

- Responding to your partner.

- Games – competition between two players.

- Dance – duets involving copying, action/reaction, question and answer.

- Gymnastic activities – sequences involving copying, matching, mirroring, using your partner in place of a piece of equipment.

Differentiation

Differentiation involves catering for the individual pupils by tailoring the teaching approaches and processes to the different learning needs, interests and capacities of each individual.

As we have already mentioned, teachers need to plan activities which enable children to undertake tasks which are relevant to their own ability levels. This will involve the process of differentiation by task or outcome.

Differentiation by task

Children with Special Educational Needs might need a number of bridging tasks, e.g. breaking down a skill into several components. For pupils with learning difficulties the skills of understanding are paramount; therefore, tasks need to be made clear if pupils are to respond.

When modifying tasks, remember to distinguish between actions on the spot, on the move and on the move with others.

Modifying the tasks

- If changes of speed and direction make tasks too difficult, an alternative simpler activity should be substituted.

Modifying the equipment

- In games – e.g. using larger/smaller balls, no bats/smaller bats.

- In gymnastic activities – using lower, simpler, single pieces of apparatus, e.g. box tops, benches and floor.

- In dance – using stimuli and visual aids to help children create simple steps at an appropriate pace with a definite rhythm/repeating simple motifs in more complex dances.

Differentiation by outcome

A common task can be set which allows children to interpret tasks in their own way and at their own level. This requires the children to make their own decisions, i.e. planning and evaluating, and can involve the following:

- In gymnastic activities – the task may be performed on the floor rather than on apparatus.

- In games – allow different ways of propelling a ball within a set area (this could be pushing, rolling, tossing or kicking).

- Rules may be simplified to enable the children to make the decisions.

- In all areas of the Physical Education curriculum, children need to plan, create and perform alone before working with a partner. Alternatively, whilst others are working in a group, they could be working with a partner/helper.

- At Key Stage 2, children should be encouraged to challenge themselves and take more responsibility for their own learning.

Chapter 6

The Process of Catering for Individual Needs

Chapter 3 suggests skills which should be assessed when considering children who may have Special Educational Needs. The first part of this chapter comprises a suggested checklist of activities, with teaching points to help teachers identify clearly areas of particular need. It would be helpful to have an observer taking notes on particular children. Observers could be a headteacher, another class teacher, the SENCO, an ancillary helper or a parent.

Assessment

The examples of activities which follow can be taken with the whole class to identify possible areas of difficulties which may be overlooked unless an assessment session is built into the programme early on.

Suggested ways of collecting evidence: observation/assessment sheet

Challenge	Look for (teaching points)
Watching/listening	• Response through action to verbal/ visual instruction • Speed of response
Being still • Standing • Kneeling • Sitting • Lying	 • Correct body stance • Head still • Fixing eyes at a point in front of them at eye level • Making sure body is straight and symmetrical
Travelling/moving – core skills on the spot • Walking (i.e. marching) • Running (for 1 minute; 2 minutes) • Jumping • Hopping • Skipping	 • Ability to walk on different parts of the foot and maintain posture • Ability to maintain rhythm • Running on the balls of the feet • Cross patterning of arms (opposite arm forward to raised leg) • Maintaining a good posture • Foot dominance • Ability to hop on alternate feet whilst staying on the spot • Keeping head still

Challenge	Look for (teaching points)
Rolling	
• Curled	• Maintaining curled shape, head tucked in
• Extended sideways	• Full extension including straight arms and legs
Body awareness	
• Making hands touch different body parts with eyes closed	• Speed of reaction
• Making different body parts touch the floor	• Correct responses
Static balance	
• Standing on one leg for a given length of time (e.g. 15 seconds)	• Stillness and no associated movement
• Balancing on different body parts – to include tummies, backs, bottoms and combinations of hands and feet	• Good posture
	• Raised parts extended
	• Ability to stand on balls of feet with control
• With hands fixed firmly on the floor, taking weight on hands, jump feet from one side to the other – making patterns with feet in the air	• Ability to support weight on hands
	• Ability to keep both hands flat and still
Spatial awareness	
• Moving around the area travelling, using different modes, e.g. running, jumping, hopping. Stop on signal	• Ability to respond quickly and correctly
	• Ability to stay on their own away from other children
Spatial ability	
• Moving about the area making 'called' body part touch the ground, either hold position, or carry on	• The speed of responses
Pattern and sequencing	
• Copy a series of actions performed by teacher, e.g. jump, hop, weight on hands, and repeat continuously	• The ease with which they can grasp what is required of them
• Tell children a series of actions which you would like them to perform, e.g. three hops on right foot, two on left, and keep repeating	• Ability to repeat and perform with rhythm, continuity, fluidity, smooth transitions

Challenge	Look for (teaching points)
Object manipulation	
Key Stage 1	
• Throw and catch a bean bag	• Look for accuracy and follow through
• Make a bean bag hit a base with force	
Key Stage 2	
• Take the ball back to your mat/roll it around/bounce it around/see how long you can keep a ball bouncing outside your mat (setting boundaries)	• Ability to continuously bounce using two hands at the same time, right hand then left hand

Challenge	Look for (teaching points)
Rhythm-patterning	
• Bouncing ball on left side with left hand, and changing to right hand on right side	• Posture/balance
• Copy a pattern demonstrated by teacher: eight bounces with two hands; four bounces with right hand; four bounces with left hand. Alternate right hand/left hand for four. Catch. Repeat sequence (to test ability to remember)	
• Throw, catch; bounce, catch; throw, clap, catch. Repeat (to remember the correct order)	• Ability to stop and be still when asked
• Using a pattern, e.g. two kicks high, one left, keep repeating – kicking the ball in between objects. On command place two hands on top of the ball, three kicks best foot, one with the other.	
• Pre-stated pattern, e.g. two kicks right foot; one kick left foot; three pushes right hand; two pushes left hand. Stop by putting one foot on the ball	• Avoid bumping into others • Ability to control the ball • Ability to keep the ball under close control using the appropriate amount of force so that on the command 'Stop' they can react immediately
• Using hands propel the ball around the area – two pushes left hand, one right. Stopping with one foot on top of the ball	

Challenge	Look for (teaching points)
Working with a partner	
• All children make up a pattern involving three different actions. Practise actions. Choose a partner, each have a turn at showing partner the pattern. Partner to describe what they have seen and to comment whether the performance met task requirement (e.g. three actions – were they repeated the same each time? Can partner copy it?) Change over.	• Look for ability to describe in words what is seen
• Lie flat on tummy, eyes closed. Partner to make a simple pattern in the centre of partner's back using fingers, finger tips or flat hand, using one or both hands or combination. Pattern repeated accurately three times. Partner to describe or repeat on partner's back	• Ability to replicate the pattern by describing or repeating on partner's back • How well can they do this?
• Lie on back, close eyes, partner place one arm and leg at a certain angle. Other child to make other arm and leg match the angles	• Can child internalise symmetrical body positions accurately? • Can child remain still?

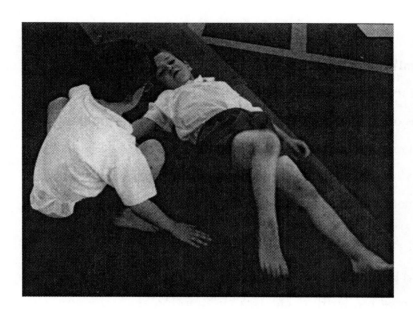

Tracking ability	
• Sit and follow hand movements of partner – use different directions/ levels	• Ability to follow both hands working together, going across the body

The results of this observation/assessment may indicate some children who would benefit from a supplementary individual programme to enable them to have an enhanced experience of Physical Education. It is necessary to recognise that to provide quality programmes for these children they need additional help in relation to:

- physical skills, including manipulative skills
- planning ability
- communication with others.

Planning the individual programmes

When planning individual programmes consider:

- Use of assessment sheet to identify needs in order to provide a base line.

- Breaking down tasks into smaller components.

- Looking at processes, i.e. expectations/target setting, use of language, teaching styles, group size.

- Independence – skills needed for functioning in and out of school.

Responses to tasks should take account of ways in which children process information, i.e. how the child learns, listens, sees, feels.

Programmes should include activities which enhance motor skills, manipulative skills and behaviour.

Motor skills

- Sit, stand, walk, run, jump, hop, etc.

- Upper body strength, support weight, climb.

- Balance – negotiation of body through space – carrying things.

- Spatial and temporal elements of movements.

- Fitness and strength, stamina, suppleness, posture, rest/relaxation.

- With equipment – kick, catch, hit, aim.

Manipulative skills

For classroom and beyond PE

- Dressing, threading, writing, etc. (watch attention span, memory short/long term).

- Patterning , sequencing, rhythm.

Behaviour

- Concentration.
- Oral communication.
- Confidence, independence.
- Learning skills – copying, remembering, etc.

All individual sessions should be taken as small group activities since so many children with SEN have, as already illustrated, problems with social behaviour. Groups of two, four, or a maximum of six are recommended (allowing for partner work).

Assessment responses

The following pages are examples of suggested responses recorded on three children with different kinds of problems during a class session using the preceding assessment sheet. The three children are:

- a six-year-old with learning difficulties and motor difficulties
- an eight-year-old with behavioural difficulties
- a bright ten-year-old child with coordination difficulties (dyspraxic/DCD) and lack of organisational skills.

For each child there follows a recommended six-week back-up programme to enhance areas of identified need.

Responses of a six-year-old boy with learning difficulties and motor difficulties

Challenge Some identification activities	Observations
Watching/listening to commands • Perform actions described/ demonstrated by teacher, e.g. make both hands touch the mat/base	• Slow to respond especially when listening. Better at copying actions

Travelling/moving core skills
• Running (for 1 minute)
 	
• Jumping
  (a) set number
 	
  (b) direction
 	
  (c) star jumps
• Hopping
  (a) three hops right, three left
 	
  (b) along mat
	• Stayed on mat and kept going but
	left leg stopped working efficiently
	after 20 seconds. Body all over the place
	
	• Can jump but forgot to stop after
	required number
	• Difficulty in jumping backwards. Can
	jump to right side. Difficulty jumping
	to left
	• Difficulty in coordinating arms and legs
	
	• Unable to do this on left foot. Better at
	hopping on right foot but body position
	very poor
	• Unable to hop on left foot. Head leaning
	forward

Body awareness • Touch different body parts with eyes closed *Static balance* • On different body parts *Spatial awareness/ability* • Moving around room • Stop on command • Use of different foot actions and directions *Weight on hands* • Jump feet back–forwards whilst hands stay still.	• Does not know elbows, shoulders. Reluctant to close eyes. Very slow and unsure. • Slow at responding but able to balance on stated part – lots of wobbles especially on bottom and tummy only • Slow to start. Tends to stay close to mat • Lots of blinking • Found this difficult. Lacked upper body strength • Incorrect head position • Lots of finger curling on one hand

Challenge Some identification activities	Observations
Patterning and sequencing	
• Flexibility/extension	• Kept forgetting pattern. No rhythm. Poor number concept
• Rolling. Curled/stretch	• Good at doing this after visual demonstration

Object manipulation	
Bean bag activities/skills	
• Throw and catch	• Can throw and catch but only throws bean bag up a little way.
• Hitting mat with bean bag	• Aiming at mat – inconsistent, use of hand suggests undefined dominance
Ball activities/skills	

• Throw, catch/bounce, catch
  (a) on spot
  (b) travelling
In twos, underarm
	• Happy with large ball dropping and catching
	• Unsuccessful moving about room

• Roll ball, chase and stop with two hands	• Slow to respond • Good but only rolls balls a very short distance
• Pattern – throw, catch, run around mat, bounce and catch, repeat	• Unable to do this – too difficult
• Following partner's pattern	• Good. Can cross the midline.
• Dribbling ball	• Quite good with right foot but slow. Not able to do this with left foot
Body tension	
• Push child gently to feel resistance	• Rather floppy
• Child lying on tummy, eyes closed. Touch child on certain body parts, one part/two parts at a time	• Good at knowing parts of body, but tends to point rather than say
• Mirror a simple pattern made by teacher.	• Good ability

Additional information
Very hesitant in response to all verbally presented materials.
Needs lots of praise.
Very slow at dressing.
Needs constant prompts.
Poor expressive language.
Difficulties in relating to others.

Programme for the six-year-old boy with learning difficulties and motor difficulties

Learning objectives

- To improve concentration/attention span.
- To develop confidence and language.
- To improve knowledge of body parts.
- To improve movement vocabulary.
- To improve posture and ability to perform symmetrical activities.

Organisation

Work with another child in a small area – increase group size to four children.

Equipment

Individual mats, bean bags, medium sized balls.

Session 1
Collect a mat and place in a space facing the teacher.
Listen to commands, e.g. 'Sit in front of mat, stand in the middle of mat.' Encourage speed of response.
Run to a target, e.g. a line, touch with both hands, return and sit on mat.

Sitting
Bend and straighten legs – both legs, one leg, alternate legs. Encourage leg lift.

Lying
Stretched on back; on tummy; rolling over for a full turn.

Bean bags
Collect colour suggested by the teacher. Practise aiming at a mat – use two hands, one hand then the other.
Use bean bag and copy the movements of the teacher (stand/sit).

Conclusion
Roll up mat and use bean bag to hit mat. How many times?

Session 2
Collect mat. Face teacher. Touch body part teacher says. Copy teacher. Encourage speed. Commands by teacher, e.g. 'Run round your mat and sit down'.

Taking turns
Run round your partner's mat and sit on your mat. Partner does the same. Keep repeating.

Knee bends
As first session (see 'Sitting') – teacher calls straight/bent (both/one). Try to catch pupil out. Pupil to give commands if ready.

Making bridges
Lying on back, push tummy up; hold for count of 5; lower.

Bean bags
Make bean bag touch different body parts as requested. Carry bean bags on different body parts.

Conclusion
Own choice of activity using a bean bag.

Session 3
Choose from any of the above activities not requiring equipment.

Running
On mat – concentrate on high knee lift. Stop on command. Be very still.
Repeat. Increase time of running.

Jumping
On mat – bouncy jumps. Give number. Make number and jumps match.
Partner to decide whether action is done correctly.

Sitting
In twos. Rolling ball to each other. Use two hands to send and receive. Count how many 'good' rolls.

Conclusion
Choice of activity, using a ball.

Session 4
Collect mat colour given by partner.
Travel around room walking/running: return to own mat and make body parts called by teacher touch mat, e.g. nose only. Be very still.

Bean bags
Lie on backs with bean bag on tummy. Lift only bottom off the floor.

Balls
Lie on tummies; face partner – push ball to partner with two hands.

Conclusion
In turns
(a) Lie on floor with eyes closed and partner touch body part, e.g. heel.
(b) Partner name body part and change over.

Session 5

Running on mats
Call body part, make that body part touch mat and start running again. Running on mat, go and touch named object/colour named by teacher/partner and return. Partner does the same.
Toe/heel walk along mat – keep body straight.

Jumping
Jump off and on the mat. Say 'Off' when off, and 'On' when on. Keep going. Watch posture.

Balls
Roll ball along mat. Use hands to stop ball going off mat.

Conclusion
Lie straight in the middle of the mat. Partner to decide if pupil is straight.

Session 6

Use of mats
Encourage pupil to suggest which activities he or she would like to start with. 'Simon says' – stamping feet, marching. Running on mat/stop; travel and stop, etc. On hands and feet, walk around mat. Vary direction.

Lying
Make yourself long and then roll over once, return. Curl up small.

Balls
Roll ball with two hands/one hand around the room; stop; continue until asked to return to your mat.
Bounce ball on mat. Number of times to be given by teacher/partner.

Conclusion
Repetition of any of the previous concluding activities.

This is only an example of a possible programme. Teachers should adapt and modify as and where necessary.

Remember:
- **the role of repetition**
- **to include activities where pupils have success**
- **to make sessions fun and enjoyable.**

Responses of an eight-year-old with behavioural difficulties (Key Stage 2)

Challenge Some identification activities	Observations
Watching/listening to commands	• Constantly looking around the room • Starts tasks before all the instructions have been given • Impetuous/behaviour unpredictable • Movement accompanied by silly noises

Travelling/moving core skills
• Running (for 1 minute)
  Add change of direction
  Number patterns
	• Poor running action
	• Poor posture
	• Poor head position, body all over the place
	• No rhythm
	• Actions accompanied by funny noises

• Jumping
  (a) for height
  (b) add claps
  Star jumps/turns
	• Poor posture
	• Lacking in quality
	• Lack of fluidity when asked to repeat jumping pattern

• Hopping – along mat
• Balance
  Toe/heel walk, forwards/backwards
•Rolling
  Curled sideways roll
  Extended roll
	• Poor posture
	• Poor head position and eye control
	• Many associated movements
	
	• Curled roll – lacks quality
	• Extended roll – no body tension

Body awareness *Eyes closed* •Touch different body parts. •Walk backwards/forwards on toes/heels	• Reluctance to close eyes • Unsure of body parts when using right and left commands • Rushed performance. No quality
Spatial awareness/ability • Moving about room • Stop – respond to command, e.g. make nose touch a green mat	• Inaccurate in interpreting tasks • Difficulty in avoiding others • Difficulty in lowering body weight • Accompanied by silly noises
Weight on hands • Jump feet from one side to the other over mat.	• Gives up very readily, finds task difficult.

Challenge Some identification activities	Observations

Pattern and sequencing
• Copy
  (a) visual sequence
 	
  (b) auditory sequence
	• Great difficulty in copying sequence because failed to watch task
	• Difficulty in repeating sequence as did not listen
	• Off task, but with individual prompt willing to try activities but experiences difficulties

Object manipulation *Balls* • Bounce and catch – two hands/right hand/left hand • Pattern – eight bounces with two hands, four right hand, four left hand, four alternate hands, stop. Keep repeating. *Copying* • Throw, catch/bounce, catch/throw, clap, catch/repeat *Fine motor skills* • High kneeling on small base (not sitting back on heels). Roll ball, finger tips only, all the way around body. Right hand does right side, left hand left side. *Spatial ability* • Roll the ball, overtake, catch, repeat three times, return to mat • Throw the ball ahead into space, catch (three times), return to mat	• Is able to do this • Willing to try • Unable to stay on base • Lacks rhythm • Stops and keeps starting again • Unable to keep going • Gets very frustrated • Wants to change ball (always blames it!) • Ball thrown too hard and out of control • Difficulty in remembering to change hands on reaching the mid line • Ball thrown/rolled far too hard and out of designated area

Challenge Some identification activities	Observations
Partner work *In twos – cooperation* • Throw and catch. Two hands/one hand. Roll ball through partner's legs, partner turn and collect. Repeat. • Copying a pattern made up by partner • Lying on tummy, partner manually to trace a pattern in centre of back. Child to repeat on partner's back the actions experienced • Place arm/leg in certain position. Ask child to make the other arm/leg match on other side (eyes closed)	• First to select a partner • Unable to work in cooperation with partner – ball thrown too hard, gives up, wants to change partner • By this time has no partner • Wants to go to the loo • Unable to respond to this structure. Dislikes being touched by partner/refuses to do task • Able to do this but very slow and hesitant

Additional information

Untidy appearance.

Poor organisational skills, always losing belongings.

Never completes tasks, poor concentration.

Often in trouble, especially at playtime.

Finds it difficult to be part of the group.

Blames others/equipment for lack of success.

Inconsistent behaviour, often noisy.

Over exuberant but sometimes in tears.

Programme for the eight-year-old with behavioural difficulties

Learning objectives

- To provide a framework/structure.
- To help the child cope – from known secure situations to unknown open-ended situations.
- To help the child recognise own needs and provide strategies for dealing with these.
- To provide a consistent approach of expectations.
- To encourage the child to plan and evaluate own actions.
- To help the child experience success and enjoyment.
- To learn to control inappropriate behaviours, e.g. shouting out, feelings of frustration, unsociability, and to respond in more positive ways through performing tasks which are achievable.
- To provide a set routine for dressing and undressing skills.
- To improve opportunities of working with others.
- To channel energies into structured activities.
- To improve watching and listening skills.
- To provide activities which enable the child to gain an inner sense of rhythm and timing.
- To provide structured activities which enable the child to gain information both visually and aurally so as to respond appropriately.

Organisation

Pre-session: Pupil to change into PE kit. Provide a changing area where there is the least distraction. Clothes to be turned the correct way and folded neatly. Teach the order of removing and replacing clothes, i.e. shoes, socks, shorts, sweater, shirt. Provide incentives.

Session 1
Base already in place.
'Go to your base and keep running until I say stop.'
'How long can you keep going?' (task to release pent up feelings of frustration/over exuberance in a controlled, structured way). Give the child specific instructions to follow, e.g. 'Sit on your mat', 'Stand in front of it, jump up and down three times'. (To increase the challenge speed up the instruction.) Teacher demonstrates, e.g. runs around the mat twice – 'Now you do it' (this encourages the child to focus/listen).

Jumping
Off and on the mat, linked with saying 'Off', 'On' (part of the rhythm and patterning on the spot).

Ball skill
Bounce and catch with two hands, 'How many can you do without making a mistake?'

Conclusion
Standing with eyes fixed on a certain spot for a given length of time.

Session 2
Jumping on and off a base accompanied, if appropriate, with words 'On', 'Off'. Tracking movement. Follow the movements of the teacher moving one hand, both hands.

Hopping
Three hops on one foot, two on the other. Perform twice, then change the order of the feet. Challenge 'Can you put this together without stopping?' (this involves planning and thinking ahead).

Running
Running freely about the room, stop when asked and make two hands touch the ground. Repeat.

Ball skill
Dribbling the ball with feet anywhere in a given area. Use right foot and left foot on command. On signal, stop with two hands on top of the ball.

Conclusion
Lying on back, child to try to be straight and symmetrical with eyes closed.

Session 3
Running and stopping on command. Challenge 'How long can you be absolutely still without moving?'
Running within designated area, return to base and make two hands touch the ground. Repeat, changing named body part.

Patterning
Start on the mat. Perform two jumps to the right of base and two jumps back onto it. Repeat to the other side. Keep going.

Ball skill
Perform a pattern, e.g. bounce, bounce, catch, little roll – chase and trap ball. Repeat.

Conclusion
Finish in a curled shape with eyes hidden, waiting to be touched before standing.

Session 4

Running, on command make a named body part touch the base and hold the position until asked to release (the emphasis here is on stillness).

Jumping
Hopscotch. Stand behind the mat. Jump, hop, jump along the length of the mat and hop off the end. Turn and repeat. Keep in the same direction and use the same action, but vary the order and number. Remember to change feet for hops. For further challenge ask the child to add an arm action.

Ball skill
In pairs, taking turns, six bounces with two hands, partner continues pattern with own ball to follow on continuously as if one pattern (this involves anticipation and good timing).

Conclusion
In pairs **A** lies on back and **B** moves partner's arm and leg to certain positions. The challenge is for child **A** to move the other arm and leg in to matching positions. Partner to comment on how successful the child is in matching the shape. Change over.

Session 5

Moving in and out of objects/others. Stop on command, or return to base.

Jumping
Continuous jumping on the spot – counting at the same time, making the number and the jump match (up to about 20 counts).

Working with a partner
A makes a bridge shape facing the ceiling with shoulders on the floor, lifting tummy high. **B** rolls a ball underneath the bridge and collects it on the other side. Remind **B** not to let the ball go too far. Repeat. Change over. (Control of force needed for sending a ball and consideration for the partner who has to maintain body position as ball is going backwards and forwards.)

Ball skill
Sending and receiving a ball in twos, varying the pathway, rolling, bouncing, throwing.

Conclusion
A lies on back with eyes closed. **B** lifts a limb a few centimetres off the floor. **A** attempts to replace the limb without resistance, i.e. is totally relaxed. (The aim is to relax and trust a partner.)

Session 6

Moving around with named vigorous action, e.g. running, hopping, skipping. Stop on command, or return to base and do what the teacher requires, e.g. bottoms only on the mat.

Jumping
Jumping for accuracy along several mats set out as stepping stones. Working with a partner, jumping from mat to mat and off the end (five jumps in total). Aim to keep a constant rhythm for each jump. Take turns.

Sideways right side leading, left side leading, or two jumps on each mat.
Jumping for distance two feet to two feet.

Ball skill

Aiming at targets. Working with a partner, aim at a target, e.g. into a basket, at a marking on a wall. **A** aims, **B** collects and rolls back to **A**. Keep scores. Set 'Beat your own record' challenge.

Conclusion

Child selects favourite concluding activity from previous five sessions. Gives reason for selection.

Remember
- **positive reinforcement**
- **to provide opportunities for children to experience success**
- **to set achievable goals for the child**
- **the importance of structure.**

Responses of a bright ten-year-old boy with coordination difficulties and lack of organisational skills (Key Stage 2)

Challenge Some identification activities	Observations
Watching/listening to commands	• Confused when given more than one command. Difficulty with visually presented task
Travelling/moving core skills • Running (for one 1 minute) Add change of direction Number patterns • Jumping (a) for height (b) add claps Star jumps/turns • Hopping – along mat • Balance Toe/heel walk, forwards/ backwards • Rolling Curled roll sideways Extended roll	• Poor running action. No knee lift • Lack of rhythm. No cross-patterning • Lacks resilience • Poor posture • Poor coordination between limbs, and arms and legs out of phase when jumping • Can hop but posture poor and generally no rhythm • Posture poor and many associated movements when heel walking, especially backwards • Curled roll – unwilling to attempt this • Extended roll – able to do this but lacked body tension
Body awareness *Eyes closed* • Touch different body parts • Walk backwards/forwards on toes/heels *Spatial awareness/ability* • Moving about room • Stop – respond to command, e.g. make nose touch a green mat *Weight on hands* • Jump feet from one side to the other over mat	• Confusion with right and left. • Difficulty with crossing the midline. • Better at responding to auditory commands • Difficulty with lowering body weight, e.g. to make nose touch mat • Fingers curl when feet move
Pattern and sequencing • Copy (a) visual sequence (b) auditory sequence	• Great difficulty when copying sequence, especially involving right and left sides • Good listening and can remember pattern

78

Challenge Some identification activities	Observations
Object manipulation *Ball activities/skills* • Bounce and catch – two hands/ right hand/left hand • Pattern – eight bounces with two hands, four right hand, four left hand, four alternate hands, stop. Keep repeating	• Difficulty with maintaining two hands on the ball – left hand stops working • Knows verbally what pattern is but has difficulty repeating movements in cor- rect order. Gets confused and gives up
Copying • Throw, catch/bounce, catch/throw, clap, catch/repeat	• Confusion – tends to only do one throw followed by a bounce
Fine motor skills • High kneeling on small base (not sitting back on heels). Roll ball, finger tips only, all the way around body. Right hand does right side, left hand left side	• Difficulty in using just finger tips and maintaining high kneeling position
Spatial ability • Roll the ball, overtake, pick up, repeat three times, return to mat. Throw the ball ahead into space, catch, repeat three times, return to mat	• Approached task cautiously. Good with rolling – rolled ball slowly, but difficulties with throwing. Forgot to return to his mat
Partner work *In twos – cooperation* • Throw and catch. Two hands/one hand. Roll ball through partner's legs, partner turn and collect. Repeat	• Last to have a partner. Throwing very hesitant and no hip rotation. Unrhythmical rolls. Slow to respond. Watched other children
• Copying a pattern made up by partner	• Good at describing pattern made by partner. Poor at copying. Confusion over directions and remembering order of actions
• Lying on tummy, partner manually to trace a pattern in centre of back. Child to repeat actions experienced on partner's back • Place arm/leg in certain position. Ask child to make the other arm/ leg match on other side (eyes closed)	• Able to do this but very slow and hesitant

Additional information
Has difficulty with dressing and organising his belongings.
Untidy written work.
Good verbal ability.
Very willing to help adults.
Reluctant to go out at playtime.
Few friends.
Lacks confidence.
Very quiet, tends to give up easily.

Programme for the bright ten-year-old with coordination difficulties and lack of organisational skills (Dyspraxic)

Learning objectives

- To provide a routine to help dressing and undressing skills.
- To strengthen pelvic and shoulder girdles.
- To improve ball skills.
- To improve responses to visually presented tasks.
- To improve eye tracking movements.
- To improve opportunities to work with others.
- To encourage pupil to plan and evaluate his own actions and relate his experiences through language.
- To help pupil gain confidence and have fun.

Organisation

Work within a group of four pupils each with differing needs to allow for building on individual strengths.

Pre-session: Pupils change into PE kit. Clothes to be turned the correct way and folded neatly. Teach the order of removing and replacing clothes. Set targets to encourage speed in changing clothes (consider the role of reverse changing). Encourage routine and link with classroom routine.

Session 1

Pupils to collect mats, place in space and choose their own activity.
Respond to commands, e.g. sit/kneel behind mat, stand on one corner.
(Encourage accuracy and speed of response.)

Running
On the mat, for one minute. Stand still. Teacher to demonstrate an action, e.g. run around the outside of mat and stand on one corner of the mat. Repeat.
Increase to two or three different actions. Pupil to say what he has to do first.

Jumping
Jump a given number of times and stop (teacher to say/demonstrate number).
Pupils take turns and watch each other.

Toe/heel walk
Walking on mat, work in twos. Partner gives feedback on posture.

Copying
Using bean bag/quoit – follow movement of teacher/partner. (Vary speed and direction crossing the midline.)
Pattern with bean bag. Throw, catch; throw, clap hands; keep repeating.
Try travelling and repeating pattern.

Conclusion
Find ways of travelling in the room with your bean bag.

Session 2
Copy actions of teacher/pupil.

Running
Marching with high knee lift. Running and stopping. Running and touching mat with part of body named by teacher and return to running.

Lying
Full extension. One complete roll over and back to start. Keep fully extended.
Lie on back, make a bridge shape by lifting tummy off floor.

Ball skill
Encourage pupil to make a bouncing pattern on mat and repeat.
In twos watch partner. Tell partner what he/she did and repeat.
Keep pattern going. How many times? Put pattern and that of partner together and keep on repeating.
On own, making the ball travel within a designated area using alternate hands.

Conclusion
Curl up into a small shape and keep still.

Session 3
Free choice of activity using equipment – longer time on this activity if speedy and tidy with undressing.
Lie on back, bend knees and place both feet flat on floor.
Push hips up to the ceiling, keep knees together and feet flat on ground.
Using a ball, make the ball go under and over the bridge, keep hips still.
Standing, eyes closed, walk forward on toes and backward on heels. Keep body straight.

Jumping
One jump off the mat. Turn and repeat. Jump off mat, right; jump back on; jump off, left and back on. Add different activity, e.g. two claps. Repeat sequence.

Ball skill
Bouncing pattern around the edge of the mat. How many times with two hands before making a mistake? Encourage keeping on task.
With a partner, bounce and catch. How many times?
In twos dribble relay – use hand/foot.

Conclusion
'Crossing the river', using two mats. The aim is to reach the other side of the room without feet touching the floor.

Session 4

In twos, copy actions of partner. Give partner instructions.

Running

Eight running steps forward, eight to one side wall, eight to the back wall, eight to the other side wall. Repeat until one step only is made to each wall.

Jumping

Making patterns, e.g. three jumps along the length of a mat; hop off. Turn and repeat but hop on the other foot. Look for rhythm. Increase complexity by varying order and number of actions.

Ball skill

Travel around the room, making patterns with hands/feet, e.g. push ball; two taps right hand; one tap left; repeat, change of direction, etc. Add three taps left foot; one tap right – keep on repeating. Work with a partner. Partner to watch and evaluate accuracy.

Conclusion

'Crossing the river'.

Session 5

Touch body parts with eyes closed, as directed. Increase speed. Repetition of any of the above activities as and when needed. Refer to cards (see p. 83) for developing co-operation, running and jumping , balance, fitness, foot dominance, rhythm, ball skills.

'Stepping stones'

Four mats placed in a line with a gap between each. Practise walking/running, stepping once on each mat. Concentrate on an even rhythm. Extend to jumping, hopping across the mats.

Conclusion

In twos, make patterns on partner's back. Say pattern and repeat.

Session 6

'Simon says'

Continuation of above sessions, perhaps showing activity where pupil feels he or she has made most progress in (a) running, (b) jumping, (c) using balls.

Practise and show a sequence using both hands and feet at different times.

With a ball.

Bat and ball sequence (only if ready).

'Stepping stones' – keeping in time with a clapped rhythm. Vary pattern, e.g. start *off* the mat, jump (mat 1), hop (mat 2), side jumps (mat 3), hop on other foot (mat 4).

Conclusion

Pupil chooses activity and gives reason for choice.

Remember
- **to relate overall aims to all school experiences**
- **to discuss with and encourage support from parents**
- **the importance of encouraging the pupils to recognise their own strengths and weaknesses and to be involved with their own target setting**
- **the security a pupil gains from repeating actions where he or she is successful.**

Ideas for helping improve areas of Special Need

The final section of this chapter suggests some activities to help specified areas of need. For further ideas see Special Needs Activity Cards (Hertfordshire County Council, 1992).

Body awareness

Children need to know their different body parts, their relationship to each other and the range of movements each has. Very often children with Special Educational Needs have a very poor sense of self. Without this knowledge, they will not be able to perform successfully actions with their limbs which require movement through space.

Establish first whether lack of body awareness is due to lack of understanding. Use visual, auditory and tactile stimulation to improve this area. Many children are unaware of those parts of their bodies they cannot see, e.g. backs, bottoms.

Activities/tasks

1. Child lying on back on the floor, touch the child on a certain body part, e.g. big toe, ask the child to say where touched.
2. Travel on named body part on the floor. Vary directions.
3. Running on a base or around the room – when told, make named body part touch the floor.
4. Travel through hoops with (a) head leading (b) feet leading. Do not touch the hoop.
5. 'Angels in the Snow'. Child lies on his or her back. Right arm and leg is placed by teacher or partner at an angle. The child tries to make the left side match these positions.
6. Child closes eyes and touches parts of body called by teacher or partner. Also use rights and lefts, e.g. make right hand touch left heel.
7. In twos, **A** makes a shape, **B** copies.
8. In twos, child moves hands together in different directions. Partner follows. Vary directions; make hands move in different directions.

Balance

A good sense of balance is essential in all physical activities. Strength and body tension are needed for these activities. Children who have difficulties with balance may find it problematic to perform such activities as swinging, walking along narrow surfaces, climbing playground equipment, standing on unstable surfaces, learning to ride a bike.

Activities/tasks

1. Child lying on floor with body straight, alternate tensing up and relaxing of the whole body. Try pushing the child over whilst body is tense. Encourage breathing in when tightening muscles and breathing out when relaxing. Encourage closing eyes and limbs feeling 'heavy' when relaxing.
2. Travel anywhere in a given area, stop when directed and show correct balanced position.
3. Standing, rise onto the balls of the feet keeping the body straight and in alignment, hands should be by sides. Hold for count of ten. Fix eyes on a point at eye level.
4. As above but rock from toes to heels, keep body straight, no wobbles. Stand on outsides of feet. Try to keep hands relaxed by sides of the body.
5. Close eyes, walk forward on the balls of the feet along a mat, backward on heels. Repeat. Reverse. Keep body upright, no bottoms sticking out, heads in alignment.
6. Stand on one foot, hold position without moving any part of the body. Count five. Change feet.
7. Kneel on both knees, do not sit back on heels. Lift one knee, bring foot through and place flat on floor in front. Repeat using other leg.
8. From above position, i.e. kneeling on one knee and one foot flat on floor in front, place both hands on upper leg, turn to look over right shoulder, then left, without losing balance.
9. (a) Walk between two lines 30 centimetres apart.
   (b) Walk along a chalk line, or rope on the floor. Place heel to toe in front. Keep body upright and head in alignment.
   (c) Walk along a plank or bench, keep back straight and feel movements through feet.
   (d) Repeat each of the above but travel sideways, backwards, turning.
   (e) Using a low bench, step onto the bench with one foot, then the other foot so that both feet are on the bench. Step off with first foot and then other foot. Keep repeating.
   (f) Repeat with other foot leading.
   Emphasise correct posture and balanced position in between each move.
10. Balancing on different body parts:
    (a) Running on a base, when directed make a named body part (e.g. tummy) touch the base, every other part of the body off the ground and extended.
    (b) As above but preceded by travelling freely within a given area.
    (c) Place both hands flat on the floor, make both feet jump from side to side, backwards and forwards (dynamic balance).

Running

The inability to run rhythmically is due to a weak pelvic girdle or a weakness on one side of the body. There is a lack of symmetrical integration. Hence the importance of strengthening the pelvic girdle. Activities on the floor are therefore helpful. A theme of rolling in gymnastics can be a useful way of developing strength.

Activities/tasks

1. Lying on back, lift right leg in air and return to ground. Repeat with left leg. Keep both legs straight. Perform ten repetitions with each leg.
2. Position as above, bend knees to place both feet flat on the floor, push hips up towards the ceiling (keep knees together and feet flat on the floor), hold for five seconds.
3. As above, place bean bag on tummy, wriggle tummy to make bean bag move towards chin.
4. Position as above, use hands to circle bean bag under and over the bridge.
5. Work with a partner who rolls a ball under the bridge, chases it and traps it on the other side. Repeat three times. Change over roles.
6. As above, but bridge position can be made more difficult by extending one leg in the air.
7. Lie on side, lift right leg into the air and lower slowly. Roll over and repeat with other leg. Keep body position straight.
8. Sitting, legs straight, bend both knees so that the soles of the feet are flat on the floor. Straighten both legs to return to starting position. Encourage lifting of the legs, rather than not sliding . Use hands by sides flat on the floor for support. Repeat ten times.
9. As above, one leg bent whilst the other leg is kept straight. Change legs. Keep a rhythm going, lift rather than slide legs. Make this into a game, e.g. straight, bent, alternate when asked.
10. As above, but when bending knees only named part of foot touches the ground, e.g. big toe/heel.
11. Sitting on bottom, travel forwards and backwards (lift each leg off the floor rather than shuffle).
12. On tummies with hands by sides, lift head off the floor, hold for five or six seconds and then relax.
13. Position as above but arms extended out to sides. Lift arms, head and straight legs off the floor. (Extending the back should be followed by curling activities to prevent over extension.)

Symmetry

Symmetrical integration is a prerequisite for isolating movements made by arms and legs, e.g. running, hopping, using a bat in one hand.

Activities/tasks

1. (a) Lie on back with hands by the sides of the body, move arms keeping them on the ground outwards and upwards until they meet extended above the head. Return to starting position. Repeat.
   (b) As above but open and close legs. Check that both limbs are doing matching movements.
2. (a) From sitting/kneeling/standing, child touches teacher's/helper's flat hands

and mirrors symmetrical movements made by teacher/helper.

(b) Repeat but copy from further away, i.e. hands are not touching.

3. Standing, with eyes closed, draw large circles with arms in front of the body. Vary pattern by alternating with large arm movements, followed by small hand movements making sure that both sides of the body are doing exactly the same actions.

4. Standing, arms outstretched to the sides, shoulders in alignment, turn palms to face ceiling. Hold. Rotate hands to face floor.

5. Standing, jump up and down on the spot, both feet working together.

6. As above, but jump, feet apart, together. Repeat, moving forwards and backwards. Keep body straight.

7. As above, but put in an arm action, e.g. hands out when feet are apart, hands return to side as feet come together. Vary arm patterns, which must be symmetrical, e.g. clapping, reaching forward or extending arms in the air.

8. Make a pattern of jumps which travel forward, backward, sideways. Establish a rhythm.

9. Using a large ball, bounce continuously using two hands at the same time. Establish a rhythm.

10. As above, throwing and catching with both hands.

11. With a partner, throwing and catching using two hands (overarm and chest passes).

12. Lying flat on the floor on tummies, facing partner 1 metre apart, one ball between two. A child holds ball close to body with two hands and pushes ball to partner, finishing with arms extended. Partner receives and repeats. Increase difficulty by throwing with two hands.

Hand dominance and laterality

Laterality is an inner feeling that the body has a left and a right side. Lack of well established hand preference and the inability to know left from right is a common feature amongst children with coordination difficulties.

Most children are right handed, some are left handed, but there is a surprising number with undefined dominance. Problems are most likely to occur within the last of these groups.

Before true hand dominance is achieved a child needs to experience activities using both sides of the body at the same time (see Symmetry Activities/tasks).

Lack of symmetrical integration means there is shoulder instability which affects posture and fine motor skills, especially writing. Such children may also have an unclear idea about direction and space.

Below are some activities which may help to identify the difficulties, and some tasks for helping.

Activities/tasks

1. Pick up a bean bag and hold it high in the air.
   Are one or both hands used? If one hand, which one?

Throw the bean bag at a target/mat on the ground.
Watch for the follow through from the shoulders. Does the child use the same hand every time? If not, which hand has the most fluidity?

2. Pick up objects, e.g. ten bean bags placed at different points in a room.
   Is the same hand used consistently?

3. As above make child use stated hand each time, e.g. ten bean bags picked up with right hand. Repeat with left hand.
   Observe ease and fluidity of each hand used.

4. Using a bean bag in stated hand, aim at a target. Use other hand.
   Check accuracy of each hand.

5. Bounce a large ball with two hands at the same time. Both hands must touch the ball each time.
   How many can you do without a hand stopping?

6. Bounce a large ball with right hand for so many bounces, change to left hand but do not stop rhythm pattern.

7. Kneel on a base, roll ball to right in front of body with flat left hand, stop and return ball to left with right hand.

8. Sit and face the teacher/helper. Copy a pattern made by the teacher/helper moving the bean bag held in one hand across the body to be placed on the ground on the other side. Pick up with hand nearest the bean bag and transfer across the body to the ground on the other side.
   Child should track and mirror movements.

9. Repeat, but this time bean bag starts in right hand and is transferred to the left hand in the middle of the body.
   This is a mirroring activity, hence the child will be using opposite hands to teacher/helper.

Rhythm and timing

All actions have a rhythm. Encouraging children to get an inner feeling of rhythm is very important. Combining a repeated pattern so many times, followed by a short pause, e.g. five seconds, before repeating the pattern, will help children plan beginnings and ends of patterns. Also use patterns which involve crossing the midline of their bodies.

Activities/tasks

1. Jump off and onto a base/mat keeping the rhythm going. Vary changes of direction, e.g. off forward, back onto base, off sideways, back onto base, off backward, forward onto base. Keep going.

2. Make body into a tucked ball shape, stretch out into a long, thin shape. Hold position for five seconds. Repeat. Vary speed of opening and closing.

3. Make a stamping and clapping pattern accompanied by counting out aloud.

4. Doing and saying activities often help reinforce the sense of rhythm, e.g. 'Count and jump'. Make numbers and jumps match.

5. Make a pattern, e.g. three jumps, two hops on the right foot, repeat using left foot.

6. Repeat above, but travel, e.g. three jumps on spot, two hops forward, repeat but two hops backward.
7. Using a series of mats/hoops, children to run/jump/hop into each base, keeping a constant rhythm. A partner could clap a rhythm for a child to keep in time with. The slower the beat the more control needed.
8. Skipping on own, using a rope, or with two people turning the rope.
9. Maintain a rhythm pattern while bouncing a ball. Now try to keep the same rhythm but travel, varying directions.
10. Using hands, roll the ball with a series of taps around a defined area, e.g. three taps right hand, one tap left, keep repeating.
11. Work with a partner, take turns, keep a rhythm pattern going, e.g. **A** does three claps, **B** does three claps. Make the pattern, keep going, maintaining a constant rhythm (in canon).
12. As above, but choose an action, e.g. jumping/hopping.
13. Child lying on tummy. Partner makes a simple pattern on child's back, e.g. one hand, two taps with finger tips, one flat hand placed on back, repeat three times. Child to repeat or describe pattern and how hands were used.

Breaking down ball skills

All children can be taught to send and receive a ball, providing that the appropriate progressions are made.

Use bean bags and quoits at first, followed by fairly large balls which bounce well. Gradually decrease the size as the child becomes more proficient. Remember that small foam balls are very difficult to catch – good hand/finger reaction is needed since they are so light.

Activities/tasks

Travelling
1. Hold a bean bag/ball, move about a defined area. When told to, make the bean bag/ball touch a named body part.
2. Moving around a defined area, keep a bean bag/ball under control using different parts of the body to push the bean bag/ball, e.g. elbow, heel. Vary directions, pathways.
3. As above, using feet/hands, alternate right/left or continuously use the same foot/hand. Change over after so many taps.
4. Travel carrying the ball, go to different bases and drop the ball onto the base and catch it. How many times can you do this in a given time?

Sending and receiving on own
Using a base helps the child to know where the ball should be aimed.
1. Kneeling, drop the ball on the ground. Release and watch the ball.
2. Standing, drop a large ball and with two hands stop it from moving. This involves bending down. How fast can the child react?
3. As above, but bend knees and put both hands underneath ball to catch it, using

the body to engulf the ball in a 'hug' catch.

4. Hold the ball in two hands, bounce the ball as hard as you can to make it go up higher than your head. Now catch it. How high and low can you make the ball go? Use balls of different sizes and textures.

5. Using a base, bounce a large ball with two hands, catch with two. Gradually introduce a pattern, e.g. two bounces and catch. Increase each pattern by one. How long can you make your pattern without making a mistake? Use flat hands to push the ball downwards from the shoulders.

6. As above, but include one-handed bounce in the pattern, e.g. four bounces with two hands, three bounces with the right, three bounces with the left. Keep the pattern going. Now introduce travelling.

Using small balls

7. Bounce with one hand and catch with the other. Change hands. Increase the number of bounces for each hand.

8. As above, but throw the ball into the air and catch.

9. Repeat tasks 7 and 8 but introduce travelling. The use of a very large ball held high in the air with two hands and bounced hard will help to develop upper body strength.

With a partner

10. Astride sitting, push a large ball to a partner with fingers facing upwards. The straight legs act as a goal.

11. As above, but bounce the ball to partner. Children have to aim at a point just in front of their partner.

12. Standing, bounce the ball to partner. Again aim at a point or target just in front of partner.

13. Throw and catch, vary the type of throw.

(See *Games Activities in the Primary School*, Hertfordshire County Council (1995) for further examples of activities with balls.)

References

Board of Education (1933) *The Syllabus for Physical Training for Schools*. London: HMSO.

Bray, S. (1993) *Fitness Fun. Promoting Health in the Physical Education Programme*. Crediton: Southgate.

British Advisers and Lecturers in Physical Education (BAALPE) (1995) *Safe Practice in Physical Education*.

Department of Education and Science (1992) *Physical Education for Ages 5 to 16 – Proposals of the Secretary of State for Education and Science and the Secretary of State for Wales*. London: HMSO.

Department for Education (1994) *Code of Practice on the Identification and Assessment of Special Educational Needs*. London: HMSO.

Department for Education (1995) *Physical Education in the National Curriculum*. London: HMSO.

Hertfordshire County Council (1992) Special Needs Activity Cards. Hertfordshire: Hertfordshire Education Services.

Hertfordshire County Council (1995) *Games Activities in the Primary School*. Hertfordshire: Hertfordshire Education Services.

Keogh, J. F. and Sugden, D. A. (1985) *Movement Skill Development*. London: Collier Macmillan.

Sugden, D. A. and Keogh, J. F. (1990) *Problems in Movement Skill Development*. Columbia: University of South Carolina Press.

Sugden, D. A. and Talbot, M. (1996) *Physical Education for Children with Special Needs in Mainstream Education*. Leeds: Carnegie National Sports Development Centre, Leeds Metropolitan University.

LaVergne, TN USA
18 May 2010
183150LV00002B/4/A

9 781853 464911